THE PRINCETON REVIEW

High School Comprehensive English Review

THE PRINCETON REVIEW

High School Comprehensive English Review

GABRIELLE MAISELS

RANDOM HOUSE, INC.
New York 1998
www.randomhouse.com

Princeton Review Publishing, L.L.C.
2315 Broadway, 3rd Floor
New York, NY 10024
E-mail: info@review.com

ISBN 0-375-75076-2

Editor: Chris Kensler
Production Editor: Amy Bryant
Designer: Iam Williams
Production Coordinator: Iam Williams
Illustrations: Scott Harris

Manufactured in the United States of America.

9 8 7 6 5 4 3 2 1

First Edition

ACKNOWLEDGMENTS

The author would like to thank Gayle Kirshenbaum for her crucial contribution, Jonathan Schatz and Andrea Schultz for reviewing the manuscript, and Liz Buffa and Douglas McMullen, Jr. for their books, which helped with this one. Thanks also go to Chris Kensler, Lesly Atlas, Amy Bryant, and Iam Williams.

For heroic deeds and many cups of tea, the author would like to thank Glen Duncan.

ACKNOWLEDGMENTS

CONTENTS

INTRODUCTION

This book is designed to be an all-in-one reference and study aid. You'll find answers to specific questions about literature and grammar, and chapters to help you with longer-term projects such as improving your reading, writing, and vocabulary. We've tailored this book specifically to the needs of high school students but it will be useful to college students, too, and to anyone who is still actively engaged in educating him- or herself.

As well as preparing you for English tests you'll take in school, this book can help you prepare for the SAT I, the SAT II/ Writing, the SAT II/ Literature, and the AP in English Literature. However you use this book, we hope that it helps you to derive more pleasure from reading or from writing, because that, after all, is what it's all about.

CHAPTER 1

Reading

READING: IT'S A GOOD THING

Some people get suited up in protective gear to read a book: catcher's mask, body armor, shin guards. With a baseball bat in one hand and a dagger in the other they face the book declaring, "Do your worst! You shall not defeat me!"

Others sneak off with a book as if it's a big bag of chocolate chip cookies. They get comfy on the couch, cuddling the book close, and savor it bite by bite, purring contentedly.

Which are you? Does it depend on what you're reading? In this chapter we'll be giving you specific tips on how to crack Shakespeare and poetry, which *everyone* finds tricky. And for those of you who would never pick up a book unless threatened with violence, we'll be looking at more general strategies to help you turn reading from a chore into a pleasure.

SHAKESPEARE

Even if you're the bag-of-cookies kind of reader, everyone has trouble reading Shakespeare. And when you're in high school, everyone has to read him; so the first section of this chapter is a guide to reading Shakespeare.

POETRY

Most people have trouble reading poetry, too, ergo—a guide to reading poetry.

MAKING FRIENDS WITH A BOOK

This section is for the baseball bat kind of reader. If you don't enjoy reading or you feel you don't get enough out of it, here's a plan to start you on your way to the bag of cookies.

WHY SHAKESPEARE?

Maybe you're the kind of dancer who does the cowboy shuffle. You know, left, bounce, right, bounce, arms kind of casually bent, head doing the back-and-forth thing, lookin' cool. It's pretty boring, isn't it?

What do you think dancing feels like to Michael Jackson? Feet popping, arms rolling, a few lightning spins, a leap, a split, a flip or two. He is *loving* it.

Say you wanted to learn how to dance like Michael Jackson. Someone would have to show you the moves and you'd have to practice them piece by piece for a long time before you could put them together and look good doing it. You'd probably have to do some serious stretching to make your limbs assume those positions and you might need some aerobic conditioning to make it through one of his routines. After enough practice, *boy* would you have a good time! You'd be *loving* it.

That's why people read Shakespeare and other great writers. It takes more effort, but it's worth it.

SIT BACK AND ENJOY THE SHOW!

Think of it from Shakespeare's point of view. In Shakespeare's time, going to a play was as common as going to the movies is for us. It was just what you did for entertainment. Shakespeare was a guy who wrote plays so that actors could perform them and audiences could watch them.

If you were a teenager in Shakespeare's day, and you were really lucky, your parents might take you with them to see the play that was on that week at the Globe theater. Perhaps Shakespeare would have just written *Romeo and Juliet*. You'd watch as the teenagers fall in love with each other, thinking "This is just like me and that boy I met last week!" and you'd cry when Romeo finds Juliet apparently dead, thinking "She's not dead! She's not dead!" After the play, you and your parents would talk about it on the way home:

"Why did they have to kill themselves?!"

"It's Love, Mom!"

"Yeah, but they could have found another way."

"No, they couldn't! Juliet's dad was a jerk. He was never going to let her marry Romeo."

"I don't know. She didn't really try..."

And so on.

Except you would all be speaking Shakespearean English, which would make it a lot easier to understand Shakespeare. Unfortunately, we don't speak Shakespearean English, which makes it hard to understand Shakespeare. And most of the time, we're reading the plays, not seeing them performed, which makes them even harder to figure out.

TIP #1: IT WASN'T WRITTEN TO BE READ

One of the simplest ways to make reading Shakespeare easier is to hear the lines spoken. When I was studying Shakespeare in college, I used to go to the college listening library and get out the recording of the play I was reading, then sit with headphones on and read along while the actors spoke the lines. It was a million times easier to understand what was going on when an actor was giving the words meaning.

If you can go to the public library and listen to a recording, do it. You'll be amazed at how much clearer everything becomes. Another option, of course, is movies. You can't read along at the same time, but at least you hear the lines spoken and the action makes clear much that wouldn't be otherwise. Then you can read the play, and having seen it performed, you'll be better able to figure out what the lines mean. There is at least one film version of every Shakespearean play—the popular ones have at least five versions. The video store will have some of them and you can rent them at most public libraries.

TIP #2: KNOW THE PLOT

Know the plot beforehand. It's not cheating, and it'll help you to follow what you're watching (or hearing, or reading) when you come to it for the first time. Get hold of any cheap study guide (Cliff Notes, for example) that contains a brief summary of the plot, and *learn* the main parts of it—by heart if necessary.

What? Learn it by heart? Oh, *man*.

It's not difficult. Just think about what a difference it'll make when you get to studying the complete text or seeing the complete performance.

Try it with this summary of *Romeo and Juliet* just for an exercise. Give yourself forty-five minutes. Learn it by heart, and get someone to test you. Forty-five minutes isn't a big investment considering that at the end of it you'll have the plot in your head forever.

Romeo and Juliet

Act I

1. Battle between the Capulets (Juliet's family) and the Montagues (Romeo's family).

2. A Capulet family servant meets up with Romeo and his friend, Benvolio. The friends learn of a Capulet party that night. They decide to go, because Rosaline, the girl Romeo loves, will be there.

3. At the Capulet party, Romeo, who is in disguise, sees Juliet and falls in love. Tybalt, Juliet's cousin, recognizes Romeo and wants his uncle—Juliet's father—to toss him out. Lord Capulet forces Tybalt to endure Romeo's presence because he's heard Romeo's an okay guy.

Act II

4. After the party, Romeo hides in the Capulets' garden, hoping to see Juliet. Juliet appears on her balcony, professing her love for Romeo. Romeo overhears this and comes out of hiding, declaring his love for Juliet. She suggests they marry. He eagerly agrees.

5. Romeo goes to Friar Laurence and asks the cleric to conduct a marriage ceremony for the young couple. Friar Laurence agrees and Romeo sends a message to Juliet via her nurse. Juliet arrives and the pair are married.

Act III

6. Tybalt tries to engage Romeo in a duel, but Romeo refuses. Romeo's best friend, Mercutio, attacks Tybalt and is killed. Romeo, in retribution, kills Tybalt, and is then exiled from Verona.

7. Romeo goes to Friar Laurence. Friar Laurence proposes that Romeo see Juliet that night and then leave Verona for Mantua until he can return.

Act IV

8. Juliet goes to Friar Laurence for help with getting out of her family's plans for her to marry Paris. The Friar proposes a plan: Juliet will drink a sleeping potion, which will make her appear dead. Juliet eagerly agrees.

9. On the eve of Juliet's planned wedding to Paris, she drinks the potion.

10. The Capulets discover Juliet "dead," and prepare for her funeral.

Act V

11. Romeo, in Mantua, hears of Juliet's death and goes to an apothecary to buy poison for himself.

12. Romeo arrives in Verona, goes to the Capulet tomb and opens it. Paris, thinking Romeo has come to vandalize the tomb, challenges him to a duel. In the fight, Romeo kills Paris. Romeo then sees Juliet "dead." He takes the poison, and dies.

13. Juliet awakes, sees Romeo dead, and stabs herself.

14. The Capulet and Montague families, grieving for their children, decide to end their feud.

TIP #3: KNOW THE CHARACTERS AND THEIR PRIMARY CHARACTERISTICS

When you grasp the main plot, you've succeeded in identifying the bones of the play. But you have to come to grips with the characters, the *particular* characters Shakespeare chose, in order to understand why the story develops in the way it does.

There are three ways to do this: (1) You can ask your teacher. He will discuss the characters' traits in class even without your asking, but you can ask for more explanation if you're not clear on a particular character. (2) Many study guides include brief discussions of the characters, describing their primary traits and role in the play. (3) After you have the basics from either your teacher or a study guide, you need to look for the evidence for a character's traits as you read the play.

For example, when a character decides to do something such as *kill* someone, you can't just think, "Oh, okay, Hamlet's going to kill his uncle." You have to ask yourself, "*Why* is Hamlet going to kill his uncle?! Isn't he worried about the consequences? Does he not care about his own life anymore? Why not?" and so on. And then, "What does this tell me about the character?"

You can't hope to understand a play unless you understand what makes the characters tick. A simple demonstration: Suppose that *Romeo and Juliet* had a similar plot, but was actually called *Hamlet and Juliet.* Suppose that the character in love with Juliet suffered not from impulsiveness and passion, but from self-doubt and indecision. How would this change the development of the play? Well, in every way, but for one thing, it would make it extremely unlikely that the play would end with both lovers dead.

TIP #4: MAP THE CHARACTERS

Once you know the plot and the characters, you can do a basic character map. Then, as you read the play, you can add to the map, or change it. Once you've got a complete character map, you know the play.

Here's our map of *Romeo and Juliet*.

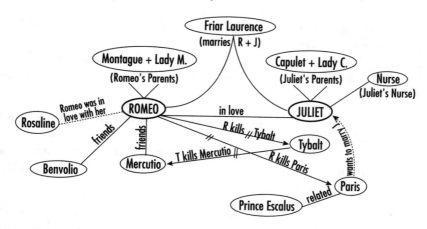

TIP #5: WATCH OUT FOR CHARACTERS WHO HAVE A HABIT OF TALKING TO THEMSELVES

It's called *soliloquy*. (From the Latin *solus*, "alone" and *loqui*, "speak.")

A character uses soliloquy to reveal his thoughts to the audience—but not to any of the other characters—by speaking them aloud, usually while alone on stage.

Shakespearean villains do this a lot. Check out Iago (possibly the greatest, wickedest, most irresistible villain of all time) from the play *Othello*. The great thing about soliloquy is that it isn't hard to spot. Just look for the part in the text where the stage direction says "EXIT *ALL* EXCEPT *SO AND SO* " From that point on, if the character speaks, it's almost perfectly safe to assume that you're being offered a first hand confession or testimony of his or her motives. *Motives*—these are very important. The character is literally *telling you* why he or she is behaving (or planning to behave) in a particular way. Don't let those soliloquies slip by unnoticed! They're vital clues to understanding characters.

TIP #6: PUT YOURSELF IN A CHARACTER'S SHOES

Take Hamlet for example. How would *you* feel if you came home from college during vacation to discover that your uncle—who had been extremely jealous of your dad's job or elected office or some-thing—had *killed* your dad and taken over his position? And that your *mother* had then *married* the murderer! You probably wouldn't know what to feel first. You'd be grief-stricken because your father, whom you loved, is dead. And you'd be horrified by your uncle and by the fact that your mother seems not to care that your father is dead!

Wouldn't a turn of events like that start you questioning the most fundamental aspects of your world? Wouldn't discovering some-thing like that (not forgetting, also, that your dad's *ghost* appears and fills you in on the whole thing), bring your very sense of *identity* crashing down around you?

Putting yourself in a character's shoes is a productive exercise. If you discover through the play that Hamlet *doesn't* do what you would do in that situation, it's going to make you wonder why. And wondering why is crucial to getting to know a character and his motivations. Once you get involved in characters' *motives,* believe me, you're up and running.

TIP #7: EATING THE ELEPHANT—WHY YOU *CAN* TRANSLATE SHAKESPEAREAN ENGLISH

Yeah, if *only.*

Translating is what you're being asked to do with the whole play. But the whole play is a big thing. Overwhelming, perhaps. There's *tons* of this language you just don't understand.

Argh!

There's a saying: You can eat a whole elephant, eventually, if you cut it into small enough pieces and eat them one at a time.

Disgusting, and I wouldn't recommend it, but as an analogy for cracking Shakespearean English, it serves a purpose. Let's look at a fragment of dialogue from Act 1 of *Macbeth* to illustrate. This is the first action scene of the play.

Scene 2. *A camp.*

Alarum within. Enter KING DUNCAN, MALCOM, DONALBAIN, LENNOX, *with* ATTENDANTS, *meeting a bleeding* CAPTAIN.

King:

> What bloody man is that? He can report,
> As seemeth by his plight, of the revolt
> The newest state.

Malcom:

> This is the sergeant
> Who like a good and hardy soldier fought
> 'Gainst my captivity. Hail, brave friend!
> Say to the king the knowledge of the broil
> As thou didst leave it.

Captain:

> Doubtful it stood,
> As two spent swimmers, that do cling together
> And choke their art. The merciless Macdonwald—
> Worthy to be a rebel for to that
> The multiplying villainies of nature
> Do swarm upon him—from the Western Isles
> Of kerns and gallowglasses is supplied;
> And Fortune, on his damned quarrel smiling,
> Showed like a rebel's whore; but all's too weak:
> For brave Macbeth—well he deserves that name—
> Disdaining Fortune, with his brandished steel,
> Which smoked with bloody execution,
>
> . . .

Now, the King and Malcom's exchange is pretty simple, although the language is strange. The captain's speech, however, gets difficult. It's a safe bet that you don't know what "broil" means here. Or "kerns" or "gallowglasses," right? Don't worry. Most editions of the text you'll be using have margin notes explaining obscure words or phrases. No one *expects* you to know what a "kern" is. The point I want to make here is that you don't *need* to know the meaning of every word to follow what's going on.

How about this for a paraphrase of the excerpt:

King:

Who's this wounded man here? I'll bet *he* can tell us how the battle's going.

Malcom:
This is a good guy. He stopped me from being captured. Hey, man, good to see you! Tell the king what's happening in the battle.

Captain:
For a while back there I had my doubts. Macdonwald is one mean customer, and he's got luck on his side—but he's no match for our man Macbeth, who's no sissy, either...

Now you tell me: Didn't you kind of have a *feeling* that that was what was going on? Didn't something about the structure of the exchange make that sort of clear? It's just that the weird language scares you into not trusting your instincts. Let's look again at the original text in detail:

After the king asks, "What bloody man is that?" we run into the first bit of syntactic confusion.

> "He can report,
> As seemeth by his plight, of the revolt
> The newest state."

"Seemeth" is just "seems," obviously, and "plight" can be re placed here with "condition." But look at the rest of the sentence:

> "of the revolt/ The newest state"?

Well, one way of figuring out the meaning is to reverse the order of the words:

> "The newest state of the revolt."

Word order was different in Elizabethan English, so altering the construction of a line can make it look more familiar:

> "He can report, as it seems by his condition, the newest state of the revolt."

Then, Malcom says, "Hey, good man, tell the king what's happening in the battle." So we know that the captain is describing how the battle went. The first thing he says is:

> "Doubtful it stood."

Word order again. Move it around:

> "It stood doubtful."

He's reporting on the battle. He had his doubts about who was going to win.

The next line begins with "As": "As two spent swimmers...." Often in Shakespeare when a line that runs on from a previous line begins with "As" it marks the start of a simile—and if you're just concerned with following the action, *you don't need to understand* the *simile*. You just need to be able to identify the start/finish point of the simile, then pick up after it's over. In this case, however, it's a pretty straightforward simile suggesting that the two opposing armies were like two exhausted swimmers clinging to each other so that neither of them could move.

The simile ends and a new sentence begins mid-line: "The merciless Macdonwald..." So if you tuned out for the simile, now's the time to tune back in. We then hear a lot of stuff about the merciless Macdonwald—stuff that's so confusing we're not even sure which *side* the guy's on. Okay, we got that he's merciless—but is his mercilessness a good thing or a bad thing for the king? We don't know. What are these "villainies of nature" and what is a "rebel's whore"? When the "kerns and gallowglasses" make their appearance in the text, we're probably ready to skip to the next page.

But!

Exactly. The word "but" puts us back on track in terms of following the general drift:

"but all's too weak:
For brave Macbeth—well he deserves that name—
Disdaining Fortune, with his brandished steel,
Which smoked with bloody execution,"

This we can figure out.

"But all's too weak" means "but none of this was good enough."

Now to dissect the next sentence, we'll rearrange the order. First, "well he deserves that name" is obvious, and because it's between dashes we'll just drop it for now. "With his brandished steel,/ Which smoked with bloody execution," must mean he killed a bunch of people with his sword. "Disdaining Fortune" means he didn't even need luck. So all of this means that the captain thinks Macbeth was pretty hot on the battlefield.

Be patient. Interpreting Shakespeare won't come easily. Try to focus on the structure of the language. Look out for the familiar words that can often explain what's going on—words like *but* and *therefore* and *if*. Sometimes those little words are lifesavers. If the text frightens you, if all you see are pages and pages of unfamiliar words, try the exercise above: pick a *small* passage of dialogue and *slowly* work your way through it. It will remind you that you *can* do it—even if you have to eat the elephant in very little bites.

TESTING, TESTING

Unfortunately, if you're studying Shakespeare, you're probably being tested on it. Whatever you do to help yourself enjoy reading Shakespeare will help when it comes to being tested, but there are also specific ways to prepare yourself for an exam.

Your teacher has discussed the important elements of whatever play you're studying. To prepare for an exam, you should write down each of those elements. One way to do that is with a chart like the one below. We've listed all the major elements of a play that you should be able to discuss. Exams often contain both short answer and essay questions. For help on writing an essay, see chapter 2.

Title and Author
Plot
Subplot(s)
Characters
Major
Characteristics
Minor
Characteristics
Setting (time and place)

Major events and scenes
Changes that occur (in characters, relationships, etc.)
Symbols
Themes
Social/historical context of the work

That's it. Sing it, dance it, play it on the kazoo. Shakespeare is yours.

POETRY

The Frog
What a wonderful bird the frog are—
When he sit, he stand almost;
When he hop, he fly almost.
He ain't got no sense hardly;
He ain't got no tail hardly either.
When he sit, he sit on what he ain't got—almost.
                                        —Anonymous

Poetry is a weird and wonderful thing. Most good poems have all sorts of hidden effects, nuances, and meanings that won't reveal themselves until the seventeenth read. Each time you read the poem you hear something new, or it evokes a new response. Although reading poetry is often difficult at first, it is one of the great pleasures of life. There's a lot going on in good poetry, so to experience it all you need to first read for each element separately; then once you feel comfortable with the meaning, you can add the rhythm, and so on.

TIP #1: GET THE GENERAL IDEA

First, read the poem all the way through once. Don't try to figure out the lines, just get a general idea of what the poem's about. If you can, read it out loud, or have someone else read it out loud. Poetry is partly about the way the words sound and you can't get the whole effect if you don't hear it.

TIP #2: READ THE POEM AS PROSE

Now you're going to read for meaning. In order to understand a poem, most of the time you have to *ignore the line breaks*. Poets tend to write sentences that go on for several lines. If you pause at the end of each line, the sentence is not going to make a lot of sense. For this reading, you also have to *ignore the rhyme scheme*. In most rhymed poems, the rhymes come at the end of the lines. If you emphasize, or even listen to, the rhymes, you won't be able to hear what the phrases or sentences mean.

Example:

> Though wise men at their end know dark is right,
> Because their words had forked no lightning they
> Do not go gentle into that good night.
>
> Good men, the last wave by, crying how bright
> Their frail deeds might have danced in a green bay,
> Rage, rage against the dying of the light.

In the first stanza above, you have to pause after "lightning" and then link "they" to the next line in order to hear the meaning: "they do not go gentle into that good night." In the second stanza, don't pause at the end of the first line. The men are crying, "how bright their frail deeds might have danced..." You need to run it together for it to make sense.

So Why *Do* Poets Break the Lines in the Middle of Sentences?!

For effect. Why do kids wear those stupendously enormous jeans with the waist around their butts and the crotch at their knees and the legs cut off at the bottom? Why don't they just wear jeans the way they're *supposed* to fit, with the waist at the waist, and the end of the legs at the end of their legs? Because it looks cool. It creates an effect. Jeans that fit serve the basic purposes—they keep you warm and prevent you from going to school in your underwear; but they don't make a statement.

If poets wrote one whole sentence per line, and didn't mix up words; if they wrote the way English is *supposed* to be written, poetry wouldn't have any more effect than prose.

TIP #3: READ THOUGHT BY THOUGHT

On your third time through the poem you should stop at each thought and figure out just what that thought means. We say "thought" rather than "sentence" or "stanza" because some poems don't have sentences and some poems don't have stanzas. Even if they do have stanzas, a stanza may be comprised of several thoughts. If a poem has clear sentences, figure out what each sentence means. If it doesn't, try to determine where each thought begins and ends and figure the meaning out piece by piece. Most importantly, don't stop at the end of each line and expect a thought to be complete. It probably won't be.

TIP #4: PUT IT TOGETHER

When you've done all that, and you feel that you understand what the poet is saying in each thought, read the whole poem through again, *with feeling*. Reading it aloud—especially to someone else—helps a lot because you have to try to convey the meaning with your voice.

TIP #5: EVERYTHING ELSE

There's so much more going on in poetry than just the prose meaning of each thought that it's actually criminal to lump it all together under "Everything Else," but for our purposes that's what we're going to do.

If you don't get what the poet's trying to express, it's difficult to appreciate all the other layers of the experience, so you need to do the above steps first. Once you've done them, start using the strategies below:

- Look for double meanings in the words. A poet often chooses a word or phrase because it serves several purposes. Finding these double and triple meanings adds layers of depth to your understanding.

- Think about images. What images does the poet create?

- Look for repetition—of words, themes, images, symbols, and sounds. Repetition is one way a poet elicits certain feelings in the reader.

- Listen to the rhyme scheme. Often there are rhymes at the end of the lines (*end rhyme*), but there are also often rhymes within the lines (*internal rhyme*). They form patterns within the poem. What is their effect on the poem?

- Try to identify what emotions the poem evokes in you. How did the poet do that?

- Evaluate the poem. Do you like it? Which parts are clear and which parts aren't? Do you think the poet was successful in his or her attempt?

- Find out more about the poet. Who is/was he or she? Why did the poet write this poem?

Analyzing a poem makes you really grapple with it. It gives you the chance to have a full, rich, sometimes life-changing experience.

LET'S DO IT

"Do not go gentle into that good night"

Do not go gentle into that good night,
Old age should burn and rave at close of day;
Rage, rage against the dying of the light.

Though wise men at their end know dark is right,
Because their words had forked no lightning they
Do not go gentle into that good night.

Good men, the last wave by, crying how bright
Their frail deeds might have danced in a green bay,
Rage, rage against the dying of the light.

Wild men who caught and sang the sun in flight,
And learn, too late, they grieved it on its way,
Do not go gentle into that good night.

Grave men, near death, who see with blinding sight
Blind eyes could blaze like meteors and be gay,
Rage, rage against the dying of the light.

And you, my father, there on the sad height,
Curse, bless me now with your fierce tears, I pray.
Do not go gentle into that good night.
Rage, rage against the dying of the light.

—Dylan Thomas

OKAY, NOW WHAT?

There's a lot going on in this poem. Poets break all the rules. They often only have a few lines to play with, and what they want above all is to get the most out of whatever words they use. That's why the language seems so *dense*, so tightly packed. It's as if the poet's thoughts have been sort of freeze-dried or condensed in some way. We need to add the hot water of our own imagination, feeling, and understanding to let the poet's thoughts expand to their full size.

"Which is all well and good," you might be thinking, "but how exactly do I *do* that?" Why not start with the first thing the poet gives you: the title. Titles are important. They're pointers, meant to prepare you for what's coming. This poem is called: *"Do not go gentle into that good night."* The first thing you might notice about this title is that it sounds like an instruction, as in, "Please do not block the exits." So we'll probably be right in thinking that Dylan Thomas is telling us what he thinks should or shouldn't be done in a certain situation. The question is, what situation? Let's look at the poem stanza by stanza.

Do not go gentle into that good night,
Old age should burn and rave at close of day;
Rage, rage against the dying of the light.

That's not too tricky, right? The first line just repeats the title. The second line is another piece of advice:

Q: What should old age do?

A: It should burn and rave.

Q: When?

A: At close of day.

What does that sound like it means? Why does he say "old age" rather than "old people"? Does "close of day" just mean "evening"? Well it *could*: Old people should "burn and rave" in the evening? Uh, no. Could "close of day" be a *metaphor*? For *death*, maybe? Old people should "burn and rave" before they die. That sounds more like it, right?

Thomas is saying that people shouldn't just give in quietly to death, but should put up a struggle. They should love life so much that they get angry at the thought of having to leave it. Not just angry, in fact; they should "rage," as the third line tells us: "Rage, rage against the dying of the light."

"Night," "close of day," "the dying of the light"—these all are metaphorical ways of saying "death." They all indicate the passing of light into darkness, the ending of a day, the time for sleep.

And why didn't Thomas say "old people" instead of "old age"? Well, first because "old age" implies something larger, more abstract, and grander than "old people," and second, because "age" rhymes with "rage" in the next line. This is a *poem*, and poems are also about sounds.

Next stanza:

> Though wise men at their end know dark is right,
> Because their words had forked no lightning they
> Do not go gentle into that good night.

My own response to this stanza when I first read it was: "Err...*what*?" But don't despair. The three lines form a sentence: "Though wise men at their end know dark is right, because their words had forked no lightning they do not go gentle into that good night."

Q: What do wise men know?

A: That dark is right.

Q: When do they know this?

A: At their end.

What does it mean to know that "dark is right"? It means knowing that death is inevitable, something that people become more aware of as they age. So Thomas is saying that wise people, in old age, do accept that they have to die, but *still* because of *something*, they don't go without a struggle. Now what is that middle phrase saying?

"Because their words had forked no lightning"

—remember, Dylan's a poet; words are actions for him, words are what he *does*. This line is saying that because their words/actions hadn't made any spectacular, illuminating difference to the world, wise men "Do not go gentle into that good night."

> Good men, the last wave by, crying how bright
> Their frail deeds might have danced in a green bay,
> Rage, rage against the dying of the light.

These good men are crying something about their "frail deeds." They seem to be crying that their small, inconsequential lives might have seemed bigger, more important, in a "green bay." What does Thomas mean by a "green bay"? I don't know, but it refers to somewhere beautiful, somewhere open. Perhaps these men feel that in different, better, circumstances, their lives could have been better, happier *and* more important. Which is why, filled with regret, good men, too, "rage against the dying of the light."

> Wild men who caught and sang the sun in flight,
> And learn, too late, they grieved it on its way,
> Do not go gentle into that good night.

"Wild men" are those who live their lives to the fullest. What does it mean to say that these men "caught and sang the sun in flight"? The sun is the source of life. Wild men are those who seem somehow to *grasp* that life source, to draw on its energy, and to let their lives express and celebrate that energy. But the sun is also a symbol of time. No matter how fiercely we catch at it—even if we manage to embrace it and celebrate or "sing" it, it's always "in flight," moving away from us. Wild men find out "too late" that they are just like the sun; in their wildness they burn brightly—but death is waiting for them just as darkness is waiting for the sun. "They grieved it on its way"—this is not to say that they were sad during their lives, but that there's a sadness inherent in any glorious thing (the sun, a wild and crazy human life, etc.), because everything must come to an *end*.

> Grave men, near death, who see with blinding sight
> Blind eyes could blaze like meteors and be gay,
> Rage, rage against the dying of the light.

This is a tricky stanza—the one in the poem that's likely to produce the most disagreement among readers. Of the many possible ways to interpret it, here's mine: "Grave men" are *serious people*, philosophers, even. Philosophers, as we all know, are in search of Truth. Now, when philosophers are "near death" they "see with blinding sight"—in other words, a sight so brilliant, so clear, so bright, that it blinds them. They see that "Blind eyes could blaze like meteors and be gay"; they realize that the truth is that there *is no* Truth out there (contrary to what they tell you on the *The X-Files*), and that being a philosopher is actually no better than being a complete airhead. For all the Truth there is to see, you might as well be blind. And because seeking after Truth is hard work (philosophers aren't generally the life and soul of a party), wouldn't it have been better to have stayed blind and happy? In other words, a philosopher might say to himself: "If there's no Truth out there, why didn't I spend my life just playing guitar and trashing hotel rooms?" It's enough to make anyone feel ripped off, which is why they, too, "Rage, rage against the dying of the light."

(Just for fun, see what interpretation you can come up with if you read "Grave men" not as philosophers, but as grave diggers, whose daily occupation would mean that they were *always* "near death.")

> And you, my father, there on the sad height,
> Curse, bless me now with your fierce tears, I pray.
> Do not go gentle into that good night.
> Rage, rage against the dying of the light.

Jackpot. The last stanza tells all. The poem is addressed (at least in part) to Dylan's *dad*, on his deathbed, or "sad height"—"sad" because it's *the last* moment his father's ever going to have, and "height" because dying is the pinnacle of experience, the culmination of all the seconds, minutes, and hours. "Curse, bless me now with your fierce tears, I pray." Which is it—curse or bless? Well what's obvious is that it doesn't matter to the poet; he's just desperate for any sign of his father's continuing *life*. In this final moment, it's not the particular feelings he and his father might have for each other—what's important is the life that makes *any* kind of feeling possible at all. It's not even that Dylan Thomas is asking his father to go on living. It's just that he's asking him to live as fully and passionately as possible right up until he draws his final breath. The poem, the last stanza makes clear, *is* a piece of advice, and a desperately felt piece of advice at that: Whatever kind of life you live, whether you die old or young, whether you're a thinker or a rock star or a street sweeper or a poet, be sure to resist death to the last; be sure to suck every last drop of life—because what's absolutely certain is that sooner or later, it's going to be *over*.

ENJOY

Try this kind of analysis on your own with any poem you read. We hope you'll enjoy the process and the poetry as much as we do.

MAKING FRIENDS WITH A BOOK

If you find reading a chore, English class is a lot harder for you than for your bag-of-cookies friend. There are a lot of reasons why people don't like reading, or find it difficult, or feel they don't get out of it what they should. If you read really slowly, or don't understand much of what you read, a book can be boring and frustrating. For help in improving your speed and comprehension, consult *Reading Smart* by Nick Schaffzin.

Reading Smart will help you with the mechanics of reading, which should make reading easier and more enjoyable. The suggestions provided in the following sections help with the non-mechanical aspects of reading. We're trying to teach you how to peel off the body armor and let the book in.

TIP #1: GIVE IT A FAIR CHANCE

When you're ready to start a book, what do you do? Do you sit down in the living room, with MTV on and your sister on the phone in the next room, and try to read the first page? Do you look up every now and then when a video you like comes on, then look back at the book and think, "This is really boring"? And when your friend calls, do you talk to her? Do you then come back to the book, look at it and think, "I don't like this," and close it? Well, if this scenario sounds familiar, you can hardly blame the book, can you, Beavis?

If you really want to read a book, you have to give it a fair chance. The best readers often have trouble getting into a book and some of the best books are hard to get into. That's just reading. The first leg up you can give yourself is to commit yourself to the first page, and then to the first chapter, in the best surroundings you can find. Settle yourself somewhere comfortable, with decent light and *no distractions*. Commit yourself to the first page and dig in, keeping your brain in line if it tries to wander. (Some people will claim they can read well with the TV or radio on. They lie. They may *read* with that noise going on, but they don't *read well*.) It might help to have a snack and a drink by your side. Give the book your full attention—if you blank out and have to read paragraphs again, it gets boring. Try to get inside the writing. Think of the characters as people you're meeting. You're being told a story, so let yourself enjoy it.

TIP #2: TALK BACK TO THE BOOK

You talk back to the TV, don't you? If you're watching *Friends* and you think a character does something really stupid, you probably say so to the person next to you on the couch. So if you're reading *The Great Gatsby* and you think, "Daisy and Tom and especially Jordan are the most irritating characters I've ever met in my entire life," say so to a classmate. Why? Because even if they are irritating (and they are) talking about it with someone helps you articulate *what* it is specifically that irritates you about them, and then you can think about *why* Fitzgerald wrote them that way.

"How do I know what I think until I see what I've said?"

A good way to get involved in a book is to write in the margins. If you can, get a cheap paperback copy of the book that you can write in, then write all your comments as you think of them. It makes the book yours, and the act of writing makes you articulate and then remember your reactions.

TIP #3: MAP THE CHARACTERS

If you find a book confusing, one way to clear up what's going on is to map the characters, in the same way you would for a Shakespearean play. (See page 7.)

TIP #4: ASK SOMEONE

If you're having trouble with a book, ask someone for help. If you just find it confusing or boring in general, one good thing to ask someone is "What do people like about this book?" Also, "What was going on at the time this book was written and how did that affect the book?" Whom should you ask? Your teacher, your librarian, an older sibling, your parents, a classmate. One of them may be able to tell you something interesting about the book that helps you understand it.

TIP #5: STAY IN THE GAME

Whenever you're reading a difficult book, there will be times when you'll hit a sentence you don't understand. Then you read it again. Still don't get it. Then your *eyes* keep moving while your brain goes for a walk around the block, hangs out for a while with that girl you like, runs through a few witty conversations the two of you might have... At the end of the page your hand reaches out to turn it and you suddenly think "Oh. Oops. I haven't *read* the page yet, so I guess I can't go on to the next one." Then you go back to the sentence you didn't understand, still don't get it, look out the window to see if the explanation's out there...

Ugh. At this rate you'll *never* finish the book.

Right. So how do you do it differently? You stay in the game. When you hit a sentence you don't understand, you don't let it blank your brain out. You take a deep breath and you *decide*, "I *want* to read this book." Then look at the sentence again. Too confusing? So what? It's one sentence. Move on to the next one. The key is not to let every glitch kick your brain out into space.

TIP #6: PRETEND YOU LIKE IT

We're not kidding. It helps, by tricking your brain into being more receptive. The more you dislike something, the harder it is to take it in. I, for example, hate computers. I've been working on one for thirteen years and it's never done anything to me, but I still hate it. I had to install a new program recently and the very idea of reading the instruction manual intimidated and irritated me to such an extent that as soon as I tried, steel walls came clanging down in my brain. I ended up reading over the same paragraph three times before I realized that I might as well quit wasting my time because I was never going to understand it this way.

The next time I tried to read the manual, I thought about this friend of mine, Jake, who *loves* computers and was very excited to try this new program I'd ordered. I thought of what he would think as he read the manual: "Hey, look at this! This is gonna be so cool! It makes life so much easier!" and so on. I decided to be Jake as I read. "Wow," I said to myself, "How exciting, a new toy! I wonder what I do first." Then when I came across instructions to "go to the File Sharing Monitor," instead of hissing, "Well, I *would*, if I had any idea what the File Sharing Monitor *was*!" and throwing the manual on the floor, I thought, "Hmm. The File Sharing Monitor. I wonder what that is? I'll go on a treasure hunt and find it!"

It's so ridiculous, I cringe to publish it, but it's true, and it works. I read the manual; I understood it; I installed the program; life is easier. Try it.

READING COMPREHENSION ON STANDARDIZED TESTS

If you're in high school you're going to have to take a test or two that includes a reading comprehension section. Reading comprehension makes up a big chunk of the PSAT and SAT; you'll have to do it if you take the AP English Literature; and if you live in New York, it's on the English Regents.

Reading comprehension tests are not really about reading well. They're primarily about searching for and finding information, and then choosing the sort of answer the test writers want. They test your ability to read *without* genuinely integrating anything you're reading. If you read well and you read a lot on your own, that will certainly help you do better on reading comprehension tests, but there are skills particular to reading comprehension tests that you have to learn separately.

The Princeton Review has developed great techniques for improving your reading comprehension score on all of the above tests. My best advice to you is: if you're taking one of these tests, buy the appropriate Princeton Review book—*Cracking the SAT and PSAT, Cracking the AP English Literature*, or *Cracking the Regents: Comprehensive English*—and study the reading comprehension techniques.

2

Writing

WHAT IS GOOD WRITING?

Arguments need to be clear, precise, and succinct. Childhood recollections can be colorful, sensuous, and dreamy. Anecdotes can be pithy or ironic. A statement of belief can be passionate and uplifting. Good writing can be of many, many varieties, and the success of what you write depends on the context within which you're writing.

Be that as it may, there are certain habits that *any* writer, whether a journalist, a philosopher, a novelist, or a humble high school student, will always do well to cultivate. There are, sadly, too many other habits that all writers would do well to break.

In what follows, you'll get some hints and tips. They won't turn you into Shakespeare, but if you respect them, they'll help you along the road toward quality writing.

THE ENEMIES OF GOOD WRITING: PRETENTIOUSNESS, VAGUENESS, AND THE PASSIVE VOICE

EXAMPLE 1:

> Undesirable tendencies in individuals are given rise to by excessive exposure to television. A leading role is played by television in causing people's capacity for sustained concentration to deteriorate. Considering the fact that it's unlikely that the national populace will stop watching so much TV, serious consideration must be given to the long-term consequences of this social phenomenon.

What do you think of that? Does that sound like good writing to you? It's got some smart-sounding words and phrases in it: "excessive exposure," "sustained concentration to deteriorate," "social phenomenon." And you do more or less get the point that the writer is worried about TV.

EXAMPLE 2:

> Too much TV is a bad habit that numbs the brain. Given that Americans love television, what does this mean for the future?

What about that? Are there any flashy words? Does it sound weighty? Which do you think is a better piece of writing?

Answer: Example 1 is terrible writing. Example 2 is good writing.

Example 1 spends 60 words saying nothing more than Example 2, which uses only 23. Which leads us to Rule Number One: Think of words as dollars. You're spending them on the clear expression of an idea. For the same item, would you rather spend $60 or $23?

Although Example 2 sounds human enough, Example 1 sounds like a computer wrote it. It sounds that way because the language is pretentious, passive, and vague.

PRETENTIOUS WRITING

Pretentious writing happens when you try to make yourself sound intelligent.

> Undesirable tendencies are given rise to by excessive exposure to television.

That sentence happened because the writer *thought* something along the lines of "Too much TV is a bad habit that numbs the brain" but then began to worry that the whole thing sounded too simple, too straightforward. After all, the longest words in the sentence have only five letters apiece—and everyone knows that smart people use longer words, right? So "too much TV" became "excessive exposure to television," and "bad habits" became "undesirable tendencies." The same thing happened to the third sentence:

> Considering the fact that it's unlikely that the national populace will stop watching so much TV, serious consideration must be given to the long-term consequences of this social phenomenon.

What the writer *thought* was: "Given that Americans love television, what does this mean for the future?" But again, the desire to make a simple, clear thought sound flashy and intelligent led the writer to substitute a whole bunch of unnecessarily long words. The new words didn't add anything to the thought: They just made it take longer to read.

Except on *very rare* occasions, strings of long words (however proud you might be of having produced them) *just make your writing sound phony.*

If you find you've written a sentence and you're not sure whether it sounds pretentious, try this simple experiment: Suppose you are the reader. Suppose you want to find out what the writer thinks about television's effect on your national culture. Which of the two examples would you rather read?

If you're being honest, the answer *has* to be Example 2. It has something to say, and it says it clearly in a few words.

PASSIVE VOICE

In Example 1, we find "a leading role is played by television." In *passive voice* constructions, the object appears first, followed by the verb, which is followed by the subject:

> a leading role (object) is played by (verb) television (subject)

Even if we wanted to keep this language we could still strengthen it by rewriting it in the active voice:

> television plays a leading role in

> television (subject) plays (verb) a leading role (object) in

A good way to get out of the habit of using the passive voice is to practice identifying it. Try rewriting the following examples in the active voice. (The answers are at the end of the chapter.) Wherever possible use verbs instead of nouns.

> **The game was won by the blue team.**

> **The clock mechanism was stopped by a faulty spring.**

> **Undesirable tendencies are given rise to by excessive exposure to television.**

> **The swimming option was the choice of most of the campers.**

The passive voice emerges when you're afraid of saying something. You're probably afraid for one of two reasons, either (1) you don't really *know* what it is you're trying to say, or (2) you know what you're trying to say, but you're not sure that it's *true*. Either way, using the passive voice rather than the active has only one guaranteed effect: It makes your writing sound wordy and unclear.

VAGUE WRITING

Look again at the third sentence in Example 1:

> **Considering the fact that it's unlikely that the national populace will stop watching so much TV, serious consideration must be given to the long-term consequences of this social phenomenon.**

It's vague *and* passive. Written in the active voice, it would read like this:

> **We must give serious consideration to the long-term consequences of this social phenomenon.**

This sentence is better but still *vague*. It's vague because "give serious consideration" doesn't tell you anything specific, nor does "long-term consequences," nor "social phenomenon," though the phrases *sound* very important.

CLARITY—THREE STEPS TO ACHIEVING IT

You should strive for clarity above all else. If you have a choice between (1) writing something in a way you think sounds clever and (2) writing it clearly and simply, always, *always* choose (2).

There are lots of temptations away from writing clearly. You're afraid because you're not sure what you're saying is true. You're worried because you don't think you have *enough* to say. You think what you're saying sounds, well, too *simple.*

These temptations are fatal to clarity. Resist them!

Of course, it's easier said than done. Here are three simple steps that should always help.

1. Know what you think.
2. Write it the way you think it.
3. Clean it up where necessary.

Now let's take a look at each step, one by one.

Step 1. Know what you think.

An obvious piece of advice, true, but it's amazing how easy it is to put pen to paper without really knowing what it is you're trying to say. If you don't even know what it is you're trying to say, what hope do you have of saying it clearly?

Step 2. Write it the way you think it.

Consider the example above. What you probably think is something like: "You watch TV all the time, your brain gets sloppy." Good. Write exactly that. It's a start. It will at least show you that there is a definite opinion that you're trying to express. But assuming you're writing something for class, the thought expressed as it is sounds too casual. You're looking for something more formal. On to Step 3:

Step 3. Clean it up where necessary.

"Too much television is a bad habit that numbs the brain." There. That's clarity. It obeys the rules of grammar, it demonstrates that you have something to say, and it says it succinctly.

COMING UP WITH IDEAS YOU NEVER KNEW YOU HAD

Contrary to popular belief, making an outline at the start *is not* necessarily the best way to get an essay off the ground. Let's say you're asked to write a descriptive essay entitled *An Activity I Enjoy.* Let's be optimistic and assume that you actually *have* an activity you enjoy. Let's say it's working on your motorcycle. You enjoy motorcycle maintenance—but you don't have the first idea of how to get your enthusiasm into your writing.

To begin, try two methods: Free Writing and Clustering.

FREE WRITING

First, write down the central idea of the essay: motorcycle maintenance. Then write down everything that's associated with that idea in your mind:

> Motorcycle maintenance: the beauty of a finely tuned machine, listening to The Red Hot Chili Peppers while I shine the chrome. Freedom of the open road. Getting my hands good and dirty, a couple of hours of solitude in the garage, just me and my machine.

> Road trips, the scar on my left shin from the spill I took that time on Route 95.

> My parents think I'm going to kill myself one of these days, Easy Rider—Dennis Hopper—*crazy.* Which parts go where, the intricacy of the machine

Get the idea? Don't impose limitations on yourself to start with. Just let your mind reach out and grasp anything that's associated with the central idea—never mind whether it seems appropriate to the essay at first sight. Just get hold of some material you can work with. Then put the ideas into some kind of order.

> A couple of hours of solitude in the garage, just me and my machine

> The beauty of a finely tuned machine

> Which parts go where, the intricacy of the machine

> Getting my hands good and dirty

> The Red Hot Chili Peppers while I shine the chrome

Freedom of the open road

My parents think I'm going to kill myself one of these days

If you give yourself enough time and enough freedom to think of all the things that *might* fit into your essay, you'll come up with more material than you can use.

CLUSTERING

Clustering works in a similar way, except that you're literally "clustering" ideas together. You start with *motorcycle maintenance* circled in the center, then attach the ideas you come up with. You can try variations on this theme, like circling the "good" aspects of the idea in green, the "bad aspects" (it scares your parents that you're out on this monster machine) in red.

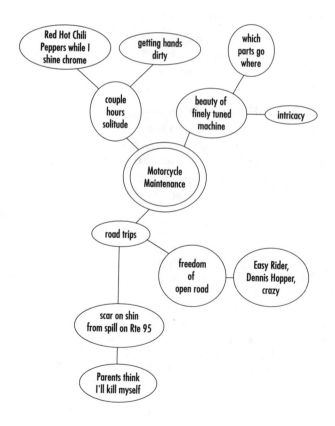

BUILDING GOOD WRITING—SENTENCES AND PARAGRAPHS

SENTENCES

Write in simple sentences wherever possible. Compare the following:

> People have different things as hobbies that give them pleasure, and the fact is that my personal preference is for motorcycle maintenance.

Fixing motorcycles is my passion.

See the difference? There's nothing really *wrong* with the first sentence; it's just unnecessarily complicated. The writer has weakened it by surrounding the point with fluff. The second sentence, on the other hand, has the virtues of brevity, clarity, and conviction. It takes the reader straight to the point in five words. Always, *always* aim for the second sentence type.

> Alone in the garage with the silent machine, I enjoy a special solitude. This is my joy: oil, points, plugs, carburetor. For me there's no pleasure like the pleasure of a finely tuned machine.

Note the effect of these simple sentences: They create a distinctive voice. There's nothing clever going on here—no long or unusual words (unless you count *carburetor*), no metaphors or similes, no technical tricks—just simple, clear, direct language that expresses something genuinely felt. Check back to my list of Free Writing ideas. You can see that I've barely had to change the wording.

Here are a few examples of what good writers can achieve with simple sentences:

> The hallway smelt of boiled cabbage and old rag mats. At one end of it a colored poster, too large for indoor display, had been tacked to the wall. It depicted simply an enormous face, more than a meter wide: the face of a man of about forty-five, with a heavy black mustache and ruggedly handsome features. Winston made for the stairs. It was no use trying the lift. Even at the best of times it was seldom working, and at present the electric current was cut off during daylight hours. It was part of the economy drive in preparation for Hate Week.
>
> —George Orwell, *1984*

Waking up in the morning I saw squirrels in the yew trees nibbling at the moist red berries. Between the trees and the window hung a cloud of gold air composed of floating seeds and spiders. Farmers called to their cows on the other side of the valley and moorhens piped from the ponds. Brother Jack, as always, was the first to move, while I pulled on my boots in bed. We both stood at last on the bare-wood floor, scratching and saying our prayers.

—Laurie Lee, *Cider With Rosie*

She would never forget how blank and pure white those corridors were. The floors, the walls, the ceilings, were all white. But once, she came upon two warders with a mop and a bucket, cleaning the floor. There was blood on the floor and on their mop. Dreadful though it was, it reminded her somehow of Christmas. The corridors were colder than the streets. The warder knocked on a door, opened it and motioned her inside.

—D. M. Thomas, *The Flute-Player*

PARAGRAPHS

What's the point of paragraphs? When should one paragraph end and the next begin? Paragraphs exist to help the reader's comprehension and the writer's expression. They're a way of dividing the ideas in a piece of writing into a sequence, and they give the reader a chance to mentally pause for breath. There are no fixed rules for when to end one and begin another, but there are guidelines.

In an argument essay, you should give each of your reasons its own paragraph. In narrative/descriptive essays, it's usual to use paragraphs to indicate the passage of time, as in the following:

I was worried that Linda would show up at the party. The last thing I needed was a confrontation between her and Doris. Doris, of course, hadn't believed my ridiculous story about where that earring had come from. That was Doris: she knew when you were lying.

Friday night finally arrived...

Or to introduce new elements into the narrative—characters, for example.

> Everything seemed to be going fine. Then Eddie arrived.
>
> Eddie Cheever was death to any party. Loud, empty, witless and oppressive, he could take a rave and turn it into a wake within two or three minutes.

In general, a new paragraph should begin at every point you want readers to pause for a moment and digest what you've just told them. A paragraph can be short or long, depending on the point or idea it expresses. If need be, a paragraph can be a single word, which can create a dramatic effect. Below is a section of text with the paragraph breaks removed:

> He did not know where he was. Presumably he was in the Ministry of Love; but there was no way of making certain. He was in a high-ceilinged windowless cell with walls of glittering white porcelain. Concealed lamps flooded it with cold light, and there was a low, steady humming sound which he supposed had something to do with the air supply. A bench, or shelf, just wide enough to sit on ran round the wall, broken only by the door and, at the end opposite the door, a lavatory pan with no wooden seat. There were four telescreens, one in each wall. There was a dull aching in his belly. It had been there ever since they had bundled him into the closed van and driven him away. But he was also hungry, with a gnawing, unwholesome kind of hunger. It might be twenty-four hours since he had eaten, it might be thirty-six. He still did not know, probably never would know, whether it had been morning or evening when they arrested him. Since he was arrested he had not been fed. He sat as still as he could on the narrow bench, with his hands crossed on his knee. He had already learned to sit still. If you made unexpected movements they yelled at you from the telescreen. But the craving for food was growing upon him. What he longed for above all was a piece of bread. He had an idea that there were a few breadcrumbs in the pocket of his overalls. It was even possible—he thought this because from time to time something seemed to tickle his leg—that there might be a sizable bit of crust in there. In the end the temptation to find out overcame his fear. He slipped a hand into his pocket.

"Smith!" yelled a voice from the telescreen. "6079 Smith W! Hands out of pockets in the cells!"

—George Orwell, *1984*

Had some trouble with that, didn't you? Too much information, too many ideas to swallow in a single paragraph. Before looking at the improved version below, try breaking up the passage on your own, inserting paragraphs where you feel they should be to make your job as a reader easier. When you've done that, compare it with Orwell's real version:

He did not know where he was. Presumably he was in the Ministry of Love; but there was no way of making certain.

He was in a high-ceilinged windowless cell with walls of glittering white porcelain. Concealed lamps flooded it with cold light, and there was a low, steady humming sound which he supposed had something to do with the air supply. A bench, or shelf, just wide enough to sit on ran round the wall, broken only by the door and, at the end opposite the door, a lavatory pan with no wooden seat. There were four telescreens, one in each wall. There was a dull aching in his belly. It had been there ever since they had bundled him into the closed van and driven him away. But he was also hungry, with a gnawing, unwholesome kind of hunger. It might be twenty-four hours since he had eaten, it might be thirty-six. He still did not know, probably never would know, whether it had been morning or evening when they arrested him. Since he was arrested he had not been fed.

He sat as still as he could on the narrow bench, with his hands crossed on his knee. He had already learned to sit still. If you made unexpected movements they yelled at you from the telescreen. But the craving for food was growing upon him. What he longed for above all was a piece of bread. He had an idea that there were a few breadcrumbs in the pocket of his overalls. It was even possible—he thought this because from time to time something seemed to tickle his leg—that there might be a sizable bit of crust in there. In the end the temptation to find out overcame his fear. He slipped a hand into his pocket.

"Smith!" yelled a voice from the telescreen. "6079 Smith W! Hands out of pockets in the cells!"

Easier the second time around? Paragraphs help. Use them.

METAPHORS AND SIMILES—WHEN THEY'RE GOOD THEY'RE GOOD, WHEN THEY'RE BAD...

A simile creates an image or idea by saying that one thing is *like* another thing:

Re-reading favorite novels is like visiting old friends.

A metaphor creates an image or idea by saying that one thing *is* another thing:

His head was an attic filled with junk.

Beware. There is nothing as debilitating to a piece of writing than a misplaced simile or metaphor. When they work, they liven up your prose. Used well, they can inject color, wit, texture, and verve; misused, they'll poison everything else in your writing. As a general guide, use them only if you are absolutely confident they will have the desired effect.

So what makes a good metaphor or simile? Well, in a word, originality. There is absolutely no point using something that you've either seen in print or heard a hundred times before. If it's familiar to you, it'll probably be familiar to your reader.

"He seemed as happy as a lark," "Math was my Achilles' heel," "She played right into his hands," etc. Boring, boring, boring. Don't ever use any of them, or any others that are completely familiar. If you're going to risk a metaphor, at least risk something *new*.

In the penultimate chapter of his autobiography *Cider With Rosie*, Laurie Lee is about to experience sex for the first time. Rosie Burdock begins his initiation by sharing alcoholic cider with him.

> We went a long way, to the bottom of the field, where a wagon stood half loaded. Festoons of untrimmed grass hung down like curtains all around it. We crawled underneath, between the wheels, into a herb-scented darkness. Rosie scratched about, turned over a sack, and revealed a stone jar of cider.

'It's cider,' she said. 'You ain't to drink it though. Not much of it, any rate.'

Huge and squat, the jar lay on the grass like an unexploded bomb.

Like an unexploded bomb. That's a great simile for two reasons. First, it emphasizes the shape and weight of the stone jar. Second, it communicates a potential explosion. First sex, explosive feelings, danger, something hidden. When I read that, I'd never heard or read it before (nor have I heard or read it used anywhere since), and it doubled my appreciation of the scene. *That's* what makes a good simile.

If you're going for a metaphor, keep it short. The longer and more complex you make it, the more likely you are to mess it up—or at the very least, lose your reader's attention.

If you want to increase your skills with simile and metaphor, read some good poetry and every time you come across an example of either, study it. See how many layers it has, and ask yourself if you've ever seen it before. Similarly, every time you hear or read a worn-out phrase—for example, "iron will" or "as straight as an arrow"—make a note of it and promise yourself never to use it.

THE PARAPHRASE EXERCISE

Increasing your vocabulary is an important part of developing as a writer. It doesn't just mean forcing yourself to read stuff that contains difficult words. It means forcing yourself to *look up the meanings* of words you come across, and then practice using them in your own speech and writing.

Paraphrasing is a good way of stretching your vocabulary. Paraphrasing something just means rewriting it in your own words. Try this exercise: Pick a short piece of good writing. Make a note of the main points and facts expressed in it. Then rewrite it in your own words. Do this once a day for a week. Just take fifty words a day from *the New York Times.* It'll force you to find several words that either share or have very similar meanings, which in turn will mean that when you have something of your own to say, you'll have a range of options for saying it.

THE ARGUMENT ESSAY

The structure of any piece of writing is determined by its content. In other words, what shape it has depends on what it's about. Having said that, it's also true that any piece of writing you'll be engaged in will have a beginning, a middle, and an end.

In an argument essay, the beginning will be an introduction in the form of a *thesis statement*, that is, a sentence or two that states your position. The middle in an essay of this type will be the argument itself, the reasons why you hold the position outlined in the thesis statement. The end will feature a conclusion, which, following from the argument in the middle section, will (at least) restate the position stated in the introduction, and (at best) leave the reader with an idea or two for further thinking on the subject.

Even if you're familiar with the structure of argument essays, it's always worth taking some time to plan them out. It may be that you have an opinion on something, but you don't know exactly why you have that opinion—which means that the middle, the "reasons" section of your essay, is going to need some thinking. Or it may be that you're aware of opposing viewpoints on the question and are not convinced that either is completely right or wrong, in which case you're going to have to be careful about how you frame your thesis statement in the introduction, because you don't want to commit yourself to a position that your own arguments fail to support.

An argument has a conclusion that follows from certain premises. The idea of an argument is that you give readers a bunch of reasons, which, if they accept them, persuade them to accept your conclusion. Let's use an example.

> **The study of history is a waste of time. Discuss in 250 words.**

First, take a position. That is, decide whether you agree with the above statement. I'm going to take the position of disagreeing. In other words:

The study of history is not a waste of time.

As soon as you've committed to your thesis statement, you've got to come up with an argument (reasons) to support it. Assuming you're being asked this question in a timed examination, you're going to have to move reasonably quickly. You can't spend forever creating your outline then have no time to write the essay. So take a few minutes (no more than ten minutes in a thirty-minute exam) to come up with your reasons. For the first three of those ten minutes, you should just jot down as many reasons as you can think of.

1. History broadens our view of humanity

2. It shows us how wars started, and their consequences, which might help us avoid them in the future

3. It shows us what's timelessly true about people, no matter where or when they lived

4. It helps us understand other disciplines, like politics, literature, art, and science

5. History is interesting for its own sake

It's better to have three or four *clearly written* reasons than a dozen confused ones. When you've made your initial list, whittle it down to three that you're confident you'll be able to express clearly. Of the above list, I'd choose 2, 4, and 3, in that order.

All you're doing in the essay itself is articulating your reasons at greater length.

> The study of history is not a waste of time. It is one of the most valuable tools we possess in the struggle to understand ourselves.
>
> In providing us with a record of human activity, history shows us both triumphs and failures. It is surely the case that the clearer our understanding of the mistakes we've made in the past, the more likely it is that we'll be able to avoid making the same ones in the future. The film footage illustrating concentration camp conditions at the end of the Second World War gave rise to the phrase "never again," which expressed the survivors' determination never to allow another Holocaust. Without such historical documentation and its study, we are likely to forget.
>
> History provides a window into the past, showing us, among other things, what our own age has in common with earlier ones. The presence of visual art, for example, in early civilizations indicates that creativity is a fundamental human activity, part of our nature. No discipline that helps us understand our nature can be a waste of time.

In addition, the study of history provides a vital context for the study of other academic disciplines. Literature, art history, politics, economics, and science, for example all make better sense if we have an idea of what was going on at any given time in their development.

In abandoning the study of history, we would be abandoning an important tool in the struggle to understand what we are, where we came from, and why we do what we do.

SUGGESTED READING

The following are two very concrete, step-by-step books:

Buffa, Liz. *Research Paper Smart*. The Princeton Review, 1997.

Lerner, Marcia. *Writing Smart*. The Princeton Review, 1994.

The best, most helpful book I've read on writing is *On Writing Well*, by William Zinsser (HarperPerennial, 1990). He's funny, he tells great stories, and he shows you why good writing is good.

ANSWERS TO PASSIVE/ACTIVE VOICE CONSTRUCTION EXERCISE

Passive: The game was won by the blue team.
Active: The blue team won the game.

Passive: The clock mechanism was stopped by a faulty spring.
Active: A faulty spring stopped the clock mechanism.

Passive: Undesirable tendencies are given rise to by excessive exposure to television.
More Active: Excessive exposure to television gives rise to undesirable tendencies.
Even Better: Watching too much television causes problems.

Passive: The swimming option was the choice of most of the campers.
More Active: Most of the campers chose the swimming option.
Even Better: Most campers chose to swim.

3

Vocabulary

If you're in high school and reading this chapter, you're probably trying to improve your vocabulary in order to score higher on some exam, such as the SAT or the Regents English exam. These exams are a huge drag and no one likes studying for them, but we hope that after the exam, when you have hundreds of new words knocking around in your brain, you'll find them popping up in your speech or writing, making it richer and more interesting.

This chapter outlines the vocabulary study methods that have worked for students of The Princeton Review. We then provide the SAT Hit Parade—a list of the words that appear most frequently on the SAT—and a list of common word roots, which will help you figure out unfamiliar words you encounter.

Learning these lists will prepare you for the SAT, but beyond that you'll find that with words like these you can say what you mean. We went through the Hit Parade list and found that there were only twenty–two words out of the two hundred and fifty that we did not regularly use. And several of those were because they refer to things—like widespread fires ("conflagration")—that, thankfully, don't occur that often in our lives.

You might think, "What kind of esoteric conversations do you and your friends have?" But you don't have to be engaged in academic conversation for these words to be necessary. They're irreplaceable in juvenile exchanges such as the following:

She: I can't believe you did it again! You finished all the Froot Loops and didn't buy any more. Now what am I supposed to eat?

He: I did not. I bought more—they're there, in the cupboard.

She: Where? They are not.

He: (Finding box behind other things) There. (With smug expression) Vindicated.*

Isn't that much more satisfying than "See, you can't blame me."?

METHODS FOR MEMORIZING WORDS

1. Mnemonics (memory tricks)
2. Etymology (roots)
3. Put It in Your Own Words
4. Writing on Your Brain
5. Flashcards or a Notebook
6. Use It or Lose It

MNEMONICS

A mnemonic (silent "m": nih-MON-ic) is a device or trick that helps you remember something specific. To remember when Columbus came to America we use the mnemonic: In fourteen hundred and ninety-two, Columbus sailed the ocean blue. For spelling we have the rhyme: "i before e except after c, or when sounding like a as in neighbor and weigh."

An effective way to memorize a word is to make up a mnemonic.

*Vindicated means freed from blame.

The fun thing about mnemonics is that the more ridiculous they are, the easier they are to remember. For example, if you're trying to memorize the word **ponderous**, which means "extremely dull" or "massive and clumsy," you could use the following sentence:

> The professor's speech was so PONDerous that I went out and threw myself into a POND.

Once you write this sentence down, emphasizing the "pond" part of the word, as we did, it will be in your mind the next time you see the word ponderous and you'll remember: "Oh, yeah, extremely dull!"

It always helps to draw a picture, too, so that you have the visual image to connect to the word.

ETYMOLOGY

The etymology of a word is its origin and development. Many of our words come from Latin or Greek roots. "Rhinoceros," for example, comes from rhinos, the Greek word for nose, and keras, the Greek word for horn. Similarly, the technical term for a nose job is "rhinoplasty."

Knowing roots can help you remember the meanings of words, and it's often useful to memorize groups of related words together. Why, for example, does the word "mnemonic" have that silent "m" at the beginning? Because the "m" is from the root "**mne**," meaning memory, taken from the name of the goddess of memory in Greek mythology, **Mne**mosyne (nih-MOZ-ee-nee). Add to this root the prefix "a-," meaning "without," and we get "**amne**sty": a general pardon for offenses against a government (an official "forgetting"). We also get "**amne**sia": loss of memory.

At the end of this chapter is a list of the most frequently appearing roots with numerous example words for each. Becoming familiar with common roots will improve your vocabulary enormously, because you will recognize them in previously unfamiliar words. Any good, college-level dictionary provides a word's derivation or roots in the definition. Start paying attention to that information when you look up a word and you'll be surprised at the connections you will make.

PUT IT IN YOUR OWN WORDS

You don't understand the meaning of a word until you can put it in your own words. For example, the word "mollify" is defined in our list as "to calm or soothe; to pacify." But we had to provide pretty short definitions, so if you want to understand all the nuances of a word, and how to use it, you should look up its definition in a dictionary, look up synonyms in a thesaurus, or ask someone with a good vocabulary how this word is used. After doing that, in our own words, we would say "you usually use mollify to talk about placating or pacifying someone who is angry, not comforting someone who is upset or grief-stricken." Then we would come up with a sentence that illustrates that: "After I had stayed out past my curfew for the third time, I had to mollify my father by staying in and studying for a whole week."

WRITING ON YOUR BRAIN

Reading a word and its definition and then saying it to yourself is one step, but if you want it etched on your brain, you have to write it down. Using your hand to write a word uses a different part of your brain than the part that's used to read, so the memory is reinforced. Writing a word and definition on a flashcard or in a notebook is vital, but you should also write at least a sentence or two using the word in context to get it more firmly lodged in your brain.

FLASHCARDS OR A NOTEBOOK

Without writing words down either on flashcards or in a notebook, you might memorize a list of thirty words with little trouble, only to find that you've forgotten them entirely a week later. That won't help you much in life and it won't help you on the SAT.

Most of our students make flash cards out of 3- by 5-inch index cards, or the bigger ones if they like to write in huge letters or draw mnemonic images on the back. They write a Hit Parade word on one side and the definition on the other, as well as a sentence showing how to use the word. (If the pronunciation is weird, you can write that on the back as well.) Then they can quiz one another or practice by themselves during spare moments.

A basic flashcard looks like this:

Front:

MOLLIFY

Back:

to calm or soothe; to pacify

After I had stayed out past my curfew for the third time, I had to mollify my father by staying in and studying for a week.

A not-so-basic flashcard will help you even more. On the back of the flashcard write a mnemonic sentence, or draw an image, or do both.

Front:

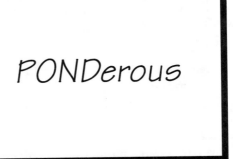

PONDerous

Back:

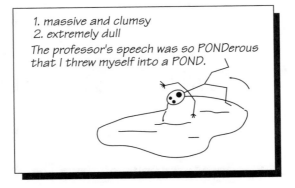

1. massive and clumsy
2. extremely dull
The professor's speech was so PONDerous that I threw myself into a POND.

Many students compile notebooks of all the new words they learn. Every time they learn a new word, they record it in their notebook. If you devote an entire page to each new word, the notebook will give you room to practice "writing on your brain." It will also give you plenty of space to doodle or jot down images that come to mind.

Even better, you can use your notebook as a place to record actual uses of new words that you discover in your own reading. If you come across one of the words you're working on while reading a magazine, you can copy the sentence into your notebook, giving you a brand new example of the word in context.

Students who keep notebooks report a sense of accomplishment when they look back through their notebooks at the hundreds of new words they have learned. A notebook gives you tangible evidence of the progress you're making.

USE IT OR LOSE IT

A word isn't useful 'til you use it. (And love isn't love 'til you give it away.) In order to actually learn a new word and not forget it, you have to use it over and over for a while. If you're preparing for the SAT, chances are your friends are, too. Use these words with each other. Pick one and use it five times in a day. Annoy your friends and family. Tell them the nifty new things you learn—such as the origin of the word rhinoceros and the name of the Greek goddess of memory. You'll get great results.

THE SAT HIT PARADE

This list of words was developed for the students in The Princeton Review SAT courses. We assembled this Hit Parade by entering into a computer all the words from released editions of the SAT. We then sorted them by frequency, weighting them to give more emphasis to words appearing in correct answer choices, and eliminating words that are too simple to cause problems for most students. The result is a list of the most important words tested on the SAT, in order of their importance.

The definitions of the words are also specifically tailored to the SAT. The definitions we've provided are the meanings of the words as they are tested on the SAT.

We grouped the words into topic categories to make them easier to memorize and divided the whole list into five groups of about fifty words each. Our students learn one of these groups every week, using flashcards and mnemonics. If you're preparng for the SAT, building your vocabulary is your single most important job and this list is the best list to study.

GROUP ONE

Ways to Speak

clarity	clearness in thought or expression
cogent	convincing; reasonable
cohesive	condition of sticking together
compelling	forceful; urgently demanding attention
convoluted	intricate; complex
didactic	intended to instruct
dogmatic	characterized by a stubborn adherence to insufficiently proved beliefs
emphatic	expressed with emphasis
florid	describing flowery or elaborate speech
fluid	easily flowing
hackneyed	overfamiliar through overuse; trite
adage	a wise old saying
sonorous	producing sound, especially resonant or full sound
trite	unoriginal; overused; stale

This is Hard! I Don't Get It!

abstruse	hard to understand
arduous	difficult; painstaking
futile	having no useful purpose
impede	to slow the progress of
impenetrable	incapable of being understood

I Don't Have Much Energy

dilatory	describing one who habitually delays or is tardy
enervate	to weaken the strength or vitality of
indolent	lazy
listless	lacking energy; lazy
sedentary	not migratory; settled
soporific	causing sleep or sleepiness

stupor	a state of reduced or suspended sensibility
torpor	laziness; inactivity; dullness
insipid	uninteresting; unchallenging

Overboard

annihilate	to destroy completely
ebullience	intense enthusiasm
egregious	conspicuously bad or offensive
farce	an absurdly ridiculous situation
frenetic	wildly excited or active
garrulous	given to excessive, rambling talk
gratuitous	given freely; unearned; unwarranted
ponderous	extremely dull
pervasive	having the quality or tendency to be everywhere at the same time
squalor	a filthy condition or quality
superfluous	extra; unnecessary

Behavior: Good and Bad

propriety	appropriateness of behavior
obdurate	stubborn; inflexible
decorous	proper; marked by good taste
recalcitrant	defiant of authority; stubborn; not easily managed

Ha-ha

wry	dryly humorous, often with a touch of irony
lampoon	a broad satirical piece; or to broadly satire
parody	an artistic work that imitates the style of another work for comic effect
facetious	playfully humorous

GROUP TWO

Things about Kings

abdicate	to formally give up power
benevolent	kind; generous
despotic	characterized by exercising absolute power tyranically
dictatorial	domineering; oppressively overbearing
haughty	condescendingly proud
imperious	arrogantly domineering or overbearing
laudatory	expressing great praise
paramount	of chief concern or importance
urbane	notably polite and elegant in manner; suave
omnipotent	all-powerful
patronizing	treating in a condescending manner
usurp	to take power by force
ostentatious	describing a showy or pretentious display

Hard-working

adamant	extremely stubborn
assiduous	hard-working
conscientious	careful and principled
diligent	marked by painstaking effort; hard-working
dogged	stubbornly persevering
exemplary	commendable
fastidious	possessing careful attention to detail
meticulous	extremely careful and precise
milk	to draw or extract profit or advantage from
obstinate	stubbornly adhering to an opinion or a course of action
tenacity	persistent adherence to a belief or a point of view

| zealous | passionate; extremely interested in pursuing something |
| punctilious | strictly attentive to minute details; picky |

Making Things Better

alleviate	to ease a pain or a burden
asylum	a place of retreat or security
benign	kind and gentle
emollient	softening and soothing
mitigate	to make less severe or painful
mollify	to calm or soothe; to pacify
sanction (v)	to give official authorization or approval to
exculpate	to free from guilt or blame
salutary	promoting good health

True or False?

debunk	to expose the falseness of
disingenuous	not straightforward; crafty
dubious	doubtful; of unlikely authenticity
fabricated	made; concocted in order to deceive
spurious	not genuine; false
substantiated	supported with proof or evidence; verified
plagiarism	the act of passing off as one's own the ideas or writings of another
specious	having the ring of truth or plausibility but actually false
slander	false charges and malicious oral statements or reports about someone
ruse	a crafty trick

If You Can't Say Anything Nice...

| disdain | to regard or treat with contempt; to look down on |
| glower | to look or stare angrily or sullenly |

pejorative	describing words or phrases that belittle or speak negatively of someone
vilify	to make vicious statements about
disparage	to speak of in a slighting way or negatively; to belittle

GROUP THREE

Oddities

aberration	a deviation from the way things normally happen or are done
quandary	a state of uncertainty or perplexity
stymied	thwarted; stumped; blocked
wily	cunning

That's Pretty

aesthetic	having to do with the appreciation of beauty
embellish	to make beautiful by ornamenting; to decorate
idyllic	simple and carefree
medley	an assortment or a mixture, especially of musical pieces
mural	a big painting applied directly to a wall
opulent	exhibiting a display of great wealth
ornate	elaborately ornamented
pristine	not spoiled; pure

Friendly

affable	easygoing; friendly
amenable	responsive; agreeable
amiable	good-natured and likable
camaraderie	good will between friends
cordial	warm and sincere; friendly
gregarious	enjoying the company of others; sociable
sanguine	cheerfully confident; optimistic

innocuous	having no bad effect; harmless
effusive	describing unrestrained emotional expression; gushy
rapport	a relationship of mutual trust or affinity

Nasty

brusque	describing a rudely abrupt manner
cantankerous	grumpy; disagreeable
caustic	bitingly sarcastic or witty
contemptuous	feeling hatred; scornful
deleterious	having a harmful effect; injurious
feral	savage, fierce, or untamed
fractious	quarrelsome; unruly
incorrigible	unable to be reformed
ingrate	an ungrateful person
insolent	insulting in manner or speech
malevolent	having or exhibiting ill will; wishing harm to others; hateful
notorious	known widely and usually unfavorably; infamous
repugnant	causing disgust or hatred
unpalatable	not pleasing to the taste
parsimonious	excessively cheap
pander	to cater to the lower tastes and desires of others or exploit their weaknesses

On the Road

itinerant	traveling from place to place
remote	located far away
transitory	short-lived or temporary
unfettered	set free from restrictions or bonds
intrepid	courageous; fearless

Who Knows What'll Happen?

harbinger	one that indicates what is to come; a forerunner
ominous	menacing; threatening
portend	to serve as an omen or a warning of
prophetic	foretelling or predicting future events
impromptu	not planned in advance; spur of the moment
capricious	impulsive and unpredictable
auspicious	promising; pointing to a good result
serene	calm

GROUP FOUR

Sittin' on the Fence

ambiguous	open to more than one interpretation
ambivalent	simultaneously feeling opposing feelings, such as love and hate
arbiter	a judge who decides a disputed issue

Full to Overflowing

ample	describing a large amount of something
burgeoning	expanding or growing rapidly
capacious	roomy; spacious
copious	plentiful; having a large quantity
permeated	spread or flowing throughout
prodigious	enormous
replete	abundantly supplied; filled

Not Full at All

vacuous	devoid of matter; empty
inconsequential	unimportant
paucity	fewness; an extreme lack of

Get to the Point

candor	sincerity; openness

frank	open and sincere in expression; straightforward
pragmatic	practical
purist	one who is particularly concerned with maintaining traditional practices
terse	brief and to the point; concise
insightful	perceptive
curtailed	cut short; abbreviated
lucid	easily understood
trenchant	keen, incisive

Earth, Wind, and Fire

arid	describing a dry, rainless climate
conflagration	a widespread fire
nocturnal	of or occurring in the night
temperate	moderate; mild

Revolution's in the Air

clandestine	secretive, especially in regards to concealing an illicit purpose
coup	a brilliant victory; or a sudden overthrow of a government
enmity	mutual hatred or ill will
heresy	an opinion that disagrees with established, dearly held beliefs
implacable	impossible to appease
maverick	one who is independent and resists adherence to a group
mercurial	quick and changeable in mood
pugnacious	combative; belligerent
rancorous	hateful; marked by deep-seated ill will
stratagem	a clever trick used to deceive or outwit
wary	on guard; watchful
thwart	to prevent the occurrence of
furtive	characterized by stealth; sneaky
impetuous	characterized by sudden energy or emotion

Put Your Affairs in Order

catalog (v)	to make an itemized list of
equanimity	the quality of being calm and even-tempered; composure
feasible	capable of being accomplished; possible
apt	suitable; appropriate
solvent	able to pay one's debts
facile	done or achieved with little effort; easy
liquid	flowing readily
reclamation	a restoration or rehabilitation to productivity or usefulness

I'll Be the Judge of That

biased	prejudiced
incontrovertible	indisputable; not open to question
jurisprudence	the philosophy or science of law
vindicated	freed from blame
penitent	expressing remorse for one's misdeeds
plausible	seemingly valid or acceptable; credible

GROUP FIVE

Feeling at Home

indigenous	originating and living in a particular area
innate	possessed at birth; inborn
inveterate	long established; deep-rooted; habitual
parochial	narrow in scope

Keep it Down

impinge	to encroach in a way that violates the rights of another
laconic	using few words

obsolete	no longer in use; old-fashioned
reticent	reluctant to speak
sanction (n)	an economic or military measure put in place to punish another country
suppressed	subdued; kept from being circulated
surreptitious	done by secretive means
truncated	shortened; cut off
wane	to decrease gradually in intensity; decline

Ever So Slightly

ephemeral	lasting for a markedly brief time
obscure (adj/v)	relatively unknown; to conceal or make indistinct
tacit	implied but not actually expressed
tenuous	having little substance or strength; shaky; flimsy
timorous	shy; timid
trepidation	uncertainty; apprehension

Status Quo

immutable	not able to be changed
mundane	commonplace; ordinary
prosaic	unimaginative; dull
prudent	exercising good judgment or common sense
tenet	a principle held as being true by a person or an organization
stoic	indifferent to pleasure or pain; impassive
austere	somber, stern
staid	characterized by a strait-laced sense of propriety; serious
archaic	characteristic of an earlier, more primitive period; old-fashioned

I'm New at This

emulate	to try to equal or excel, especially through imitation
naive	lacking sophistication
nascent	coming into existence; emerging
novice	a beginner

Things That Suck

toxic	poisonous
brittle	easily broken when subjected to pressure
malice	extreme ill will or spite
malfeasance	misconduct or wrongdoing, especially by a public official

New and Different

dilettante	a dabbler in or one who superficially understands an art or a field of knowledge
disparate	fundamentally distinct or different
eclectic	made up of a variety of sources or styles
genre	describing a category of artistic endeavor
novel	strikingly new, unusual, or different
epiphany	a sudden burst of understanding or discovery
whimsical	subject to erratic behavior; unpredictable

Emotional

poignant	profoundly moving; touching
lament	to express grief for; mourn
intuitive	knowing or perceiving quickly and readily

THE ROOT PARADE

When you look up the definition of a word on this list, try to relate that definition to the root. Some students go through this list one root at a time. They look up all the words under one root and learn the definitions together. As always, whatever works for you is best.

To show you how each root relates to words you already know, each list includes an easy word or two. For example, the letters "spic" come from a Latin word meaning to look or see, as in the easy words conspicuous and suspicious. Recognizing that will help you memorize the definition of the difficult word auspicious, which is on the same list. And you thought you didn't know Latin!

You will notice that the same root can be spelled in different ways. We have included the most common spelling variations in the heading. Remember that roots tell us the common heritage of words thousands of years old, and over the centuries spelling variations occur.

A (without)
amoral
atheist
atypical
anonymous
apathy
amorphous
atrophy
apartheid
anomaly
agnostic

AB/ABS (off, away from, apart, down)
abduct
abhor
abolish
abstract
abnormal
abdicate

abstinent
absolution
abstruse
abrogate
abscond
abjure
abstemious
ablution
abominate
aberrant

AC/ACR (sharp, bitter)
acid
acute
acerbic
exacerbate
acrid
acrimonious
acumen

ACT/AG (to do, to drive, to force, to lead)
- act
- agent
- agile
- agitate
- exacting
- litigate
- prodigal
- prodigious
- pedagogue
- demagogue
- synagogue
- cogent
- exigent

AD/AL (to, toward, near)
- adapt
- adjacent
- addict
- admire
- address
- adhere
- administer
- adore
- advice
- adjoin
- adultery
- advocate
- allure
- alloy

AL/ALI/ALTER (other, another)
- alternative
- alias
- alibi
- alien

- alter ego
- alienation
- altruist
- altercation
- allegory

AM (love)
- amateur
- amatory
- amorous
- enamored
- amity
- paramour
- inamorata
- amiable
- amicable

AMB (to go, to walk)
- ambitious
- amble
- preamble
- ambulance
- ambulatory
- perambulator
- circumambulate

AMB/AMPH (around)
- amphitheater
- ambit
- ambience
- ambient

AMB/AMPH (both, more than one)
- ambiguous
- amphibian
- ambivalent
- ambidextrous

ANIM (life, mind, soul, spirit)
- unanimous
- animosity
- equanimity
- magnanimous
- pusillanimous

ANTE (before)
- ante
- anterior
- antecedent
- antedate
- antebellum
- antediluvian

ANTHRO/ANDR (man, human)
- anthropology
- android
- misanthrope
- philanthropy
- anthropomorphic
- philander
- androgynous
- anthropocentric

ANNU/ENNI (year)
- annual
- anniversary
- biannual
- biennial
- centennial
- annuity
- perennial
- annals
- millennium

ANTI (against)
- antidote
- antiseptic
- antipathy
- antipodal

APO (away)
- apology
- apostle
- apocalypse
- apogee
- apocryphal
- apotheosis
- apostasy
- apoplexy

APT/EPT (skill, fitness, ability)
- adapt
- aptitude
- apt
- inept
- adept

ARCH/ARCHI (chief, principal)
- architect
- archenemy
- archetype
- archipelago

ARCHY (ruler)
- monarchy
- matriarchy
- patriarchy
- anarchy
- hierarchy
- oligarchy

ART (skill, craft)
- art
- artificial

artifice
artisan
artifact
artful
artless

AUC/AUG/AUX (to increase)
auction
auxiliary
augment
august

AUTO (self)
automatic
autopsy
autocrat
autonomy

BE (to be, to have a certain quality)
belittle
belated
bemoan
befriend
bewilder
begrudge
bequeath
bespeak
belie
beguile
beset
bemuse
bereft

BEL/BELL (war)
rebel
belligerent
bellicose
antebellum

BEN/BON (good)
benefit
beneficiary
beneficent
benefactor
benign
benevolent
benediction
bonus
bon vivant
bona fide

BI (twice, doubly)
binoculars
biannual
biennial
bigamy
bilateral
bilingual
bipartisan

BRI/BREV (brief, short)
brief
abbreviate
abridge
brevity

CAD/CID (to fall, to happen by chance)
accident
coincidence
decadent
cascade
recidivism
cadence

CAND (to burn)
candle
incandescent
candor

CANT/CENT/CHANT (to sing)

chant
enchant
accent
recant
incantation
incentive

CAP/CIP/CEPT (to take, to get)

capture
anticipate
intercept
susceptible
emancipate
recipient
incipient
percipient
precept

CAP/CAPIT/CIPIT (head, headlong)

capital
cape
captain
disciple
principle
principal
precipice
precipitate
precipitous
capitulate
capitalism
precipitation
caption
recapitulate

CARD/CORD/COUR (heart)

cardiac
courage
encourage
concord
discord
accord
concordance
cordial

CARN (flesh)

carnivorous
carnival
carnal
carnage
reincarnation
incarnation

CAST/CHAST (cut)

caste
castigate
chastise
chaste

CAUST (to burn)

caustic
holocaust

CED/CEED/CESS (to go, to yield, to stop)

exceed
precede
recess
concede
cede
access
predecessor
precedent
antecedent

recede
abscess
cessation
incessant

CENTR (center)
central
concentrate
eccentric
concentric
centrifuge
egocentric

CERN/CERT/CRET/ CRIM/CRIT (to separate, to judge, to distinguish, to decide)
concern
critic
secret
crime
discrete
ascertain
certitude
hypocrite
discriminate
criterion
discern
recrimination

CHRON (time)
synchronize
chronicle
chronology
chronic
chronological
anachronism
chronometer

CIRCU (around, on all sides)
circumference
circumstances
circuit
circumspect
circumvent
circumnavigate
circumambulate
circumlocution
circumscribe
circuitous

CIS (to cut)
scissors
precise
exorcise
excise
incision
incisive
concise

CIT (to set in motion)
excite
incite
solicit
solicitous

CLA/CLO/CLU (shut, close)
closet
enclose
conclude
claustrophobia
disclose
exclusive
recluse
preclude
seclude
cloister
foreclose

CLAIM/CLAM (to shout, to cry out)
exclaim
proclaim
acclaim
clamor
disclaim
reclaim
declaim

CLI (to lean toward)
decline
recline
climax
proclivity
disinclination

CO/COL/COM/CON (with, together)
connect
confide
concede
coerce
cohesive
cohort
confederate
collaborate
compatible
coherent
comply
conjugal
connubial
congenial
convivial
coalesce
coalition
contrite
conciliate
conclave
commensurate

CRAT/CRACY (to govern)
bureaucracy
democracy
aristocracy
theocracy
plutocracy
autocracy

CRE/CRESC/CRET (to grow)
creation
increase
crescendo
increment
accretion
accrue

CRED (to believe, to trust)
incredible
credibility
credentials
credit
creed
credo
credence
credulity
incredulous

CRYP (hidden)
crypt
cryptic
apocryphal
cryptography

CUB/CUMB (to lie down)
cubicle
succumb
incubate

CULP (blame)
culprit
culpable
exculpate
inculpate
mea culpa

COUR/CUR (running, a course)
occur
recur
current
curriculum
courier
cursive
excursion
concur
concurrent
incur
incursion
discourse
discursive
precursor
recourse
cursory

DE (away, off, down, completely, reversal)
descend
detract
decipher
deface
defile
defraud
deplete
denounce
decry
defer
defame
delineate
deferential

DEM (people)
democracy
epidemic
endemic
demagogue
demographics
pandemic

DI/DIA (apart, through)
dialogue
diagnose
diameter
dilate
digress
dilatory
diaphanous
dichotomy
dialectic

DIC/DICT/DIT (to say, to tell, to use words)
dictionary
dictate
predict
contradict
verdict
abdicate
edict
dictum
malediction
benediction
indict
indite
diction
interdict
obiter dictum

DIGN (worth)
dignity
dignitary

dignify
deign
indignant
condign
disdain
infra dig

DIS/DIF (away from, apart, reversal, not)
disperse
disseminate
dissipate
dissuade
diffuse

DAC/DOC (to teach)
doctor
doctrine
indoctrinate
doctrinaire
docile
didactic

DOG/DOX (opinion)
orthodox
paradox
dogma
dogmatic

DOL (suffer, pain)
condolence
indolence
doleful
dolorous

DON/DOT/DOW (to give)
donate
donor
pardon

condone
antidote
anecdote
endow
dowry

DUB (doubt)
dubious
dubiety
indubitable

DUC/DUCT (to lead)
conduct
abduct
conducive
seduce
induct
induce
ductile

DUR (hard)
endure
durable
duress
dour
obdurate

DYS (faulty)
dysfunction
dystopia
dyspepsia
dyslexia

EPI (upon)
epidemic
epilogue
epidermis
epistle
epitome
epigram

epithet
epitaph

EQU (equal, even)
equation
adequate
equivalent
equilibrium
equable
equidistant
equity
iniquity
equanimity
equivocate
equivocal

ERR (to wander)
err
error
erratic
erroneous
errant
aberrant

ESCE (becoming)
adolescent
obsolescent
iridescent
luminescent
coalesce
quiescent
acquiescent
effervescent
incandescent
evanescent
convalescent
reminiscent

EU (good, well)
euphoria
euphemism
eulogy
eugenics
euthanasia
euphony

E/EF/EX (out, out of, from, former, completely)
evade
exclude
extricate
exonerate
extort
exhort
expire
exalt
exult
effervesce
extenuate
efface
effusion
egregious

EXTRA (outside of, beyond)
extraordinary
extrasensory
extraneous
extrapolate

FAB/FAM (speak)
fable
fabulous
affable
ineffable
fame
famous

defame

infamous

FAC/FIC/FIG/FAIT/FEIT/FY (to do, to make)

factory

facsimile

benefactor

facile

faction

fiction

factitious

efficient

deficient

proficient

munificent

prolific

soporific

figure

figment

configuration

effigy

magnify

rarefy

ratify

ramification

counterfeit

feign

fait accompli

ex post facto

FER (to bring, to carry, to bear)

offer

transfer

confer

referendum

infer

fertile

proffer

defer

proliferate

vociferous

FERV (to boil, to bubble, to burn)

fervor

fervid

effervescent

FID (faith, trust)

confide

confident

confidant

affidavit

diffident

fidelity

infidelity

perfidy

fiduciary

infidel

semper fidelis

bona fide

FIN (end)

final

finale

confine

define

definitive

infinite

affinity

infinitesimal

FLAG/FLAM (to burn)

flame

flamboyant

flammable

inflammatory
flagrant
conflagration
in flagrante delicto

FLECT/FLEX (to bend)
deflect
flexible
inflect
reflect
genuflect

FLICT (to strike)
afflict
inflict
conflict
profligate

FLU, FLUX (to flow)
fluid
influence
fluent
affluent
fluctuation
influx
effluence
confluence
superfluous
mellifluous

FORE (before)
foresight
foreshadow
forestall
forgo
forbear

FORT (chance)
fortune
fortunate
fortuitous

FRA/FRAC/FRAG/ FRING (to break)
fracture
fraction
fragment
fragile
refraction
fractious
infraction
refractory
infringe

FRUIT/FRUG (fruit, produce)
fruitful
fruition
frugal

FUND/FOUND (bottom)
foundation
fundamental
founder
profound

FUS (to pour)
confuse
transfusion
profuse
effusive
diffuse
suffuse
infusion

GEN (birth, creation, race, kind)
generous
generate
genetics
photogenic
degenerate

homogeneous
genealogy
gender
genre
genesis
carcinogenic
genial
congenial
ingenuous
ingenue
indigenous
congenital
progeny
engender
miscegenation
sui generis

GN/GNO (know)
ignore
ignoramus
recognize
incognito
diagnose
prognosis
agnostic
cognitive
cognoscent
cognizant

GRAND (big)
grand
grandeur
grandiose
aggrandize
grandiloquent

GRAT (pleasing)
grateful
ingrate
ingratiate

gratuity
gratuitous

GRAV/GRIEV (heavy, serious)
grave
grief
aggrieve
gravity
grievous

GREG (herd)
congregation
segregation
aggregation
gregarious
egregious

GRAD/GRESS (to step)
progress
graduate
gradual
aggressive
regress
degrade
retrograde
transgress
digress
egress

HER/HES (to stick)
coherent
cohesive
adhesive
adherent
inherent

(H)ETERO (different)
heterosexual
heterogeneous
heterodox

(H)OM (same)
homogeneous
homonym
homosexual
anomaly
homeostasis

HYPER (over, excessive)
hyperactive
hyperbole

HYPO (under, beneath, less than)
hypodermic
hypochondriac
hypothesis
hypocritical

ID (one's own)
idiot
idiom
idiosyncrasy

IM/IN/EM/EN (in, into)
in
embrace
enclose
ingratiate
intrinsic
influx
incarnate
implicit
indigenous

IM/IN (not, without)
inactive
indifferent
innocuous
insipid
indolence

impartial
inept
indigent

INFRA (beneath)
infrastructure
infrared
infrasonic

INTER (between, among)
interstate
interim
interloper
interlude
intermittent
interplay
intersperse
intervene

INTRA (within)
intramural
intrastate
intravenous

JECT (to throw, to throw down)
inject
eject
project
trajectory
conjecture
dejected
abject

JOIN/JUNCT (to meet, to join)
junction
joint
adjoin

subjugate
juxtapose
injunction
rejoinder
conjugal
junta

JUR (to swear)
jury
perjury
abjure
adjure

LECT/LEG (to select, to choose)
collect
elect
select
electorate
predilection
eclectic
elegant

LEV (lift, light, rise)
elevator
relieve
lever
alleviate
levitate
relevant
levee
levity

LOC/LOG/LOQU (word, speech)
dialogue
eloquent
elocution
locution
interlocutor

prologue
epilogue
soliloquy
eulogy
colloquial
grandiloquent
philology
neologism
tautology
loquacious

LUC/LUM/LUS (light)
illustrate
illuminate
luminous
luminescent
illustrious
lackluster
translucent
lucid
elucidate

LUD/LUS (to play)
illusion
ludicrous
delude
elude
elusive
allude
collusion
prelude
interlude

LUT/LUG/LUV (to wash)
lavatory
dilute
pollute
deluge
antediluvian

MAG/MAJ/MAX (big)

magnify
magnitude
major
maximum
majestic
magnanimous
magnate
maxim
magniloquent

MAL/MALE (bad, ill, evil, wrong)

malfunction
malodorous
malicious
malcontent
malign
malaise
dismal
malapropism
maladroit
malevolent
malinger
malfeasance
malefactor
malediction

MAN (hand)

manual
manufacture
emancipate
manifest
mandate
mandatory

MATER/MATR (woman, mother)

matrimony
maternal
maternity
matriculate
matriarch

MIN (small)

minute
minutiae
diminution
miniature
diminish

MIN (to project, to hang over)

eminent
imminent
prominent
preeminent

MIS/MIT (to send)

transmit
manumit
emissary
missive
intermittent
remit
remission
demise

MISC (mixed)

miscellaneous
miscegenation
promiscuous

MON/MONIT (to warn)

monument
monitor

summons
admonish
remonstrate

MORPH (shape)

amorphous
metamorphosis
polymorphous
anthropomorphic

MORT (death)

immortal
morgue
morbid
moribund
mortify

MUT (change)

commute
mutation
mutant
immutable
transmutation
permutation

NAM/NOM/NOUN/ NOWN/NYM (rule, order)

astronomy
economy
autonomy
antimony
gastronomy
taxonomy

NAT/NAS/NAI (to be born)

natural
native
naive

cognate
nascent
innate
renaissance

NEC/NIC/NOC/NOX (harm, death)

innocent
noxious
obnoxious
pernicious
internecine
innocuous
necromancy

NOM/NYM/NOUN/ NOWN (name)

synonym
anonymous
nominate
pseudonym
misnomer
nomenclature
acronym
homonym
nominal
ignominy
denomination
noun
renown
nom de plume
nom de guerre

NOV/NEO/NOU (new)

novice
novel
novelty
renovate
innovate

neologism
neophyte
nouvelle cuisine
nouveau riche

NOUNC/NUNC (to announce)
announce
pronounce
denounce
renounce

OB/OC/OF/OP (toward, to, against, completely, over)
obese
object
obstruct
obstinate
obscure
obtrude
oblique
oblivious
obnoxious
obstreperous
obtuse
opprobrium
obsequious
obfuscate

OMNI (all)
omnipresent
omniscient
omnipotent

PAC/PEAC (peace)
peace
appease
pacify
pacifist

pacifier
pact

PAN (all, everywhere)
panorama
panacea
panegyric
pantheon
panoply
pandemic

PAR (equal)
par
parity
apartheid
disparity
disparate
disparage

PARA (next to, beside)
parallel
paraphrase
parasite
paradox
parody
paragon
parable
paradigm
paramilitary
paranoid
paranormal
parapsychology
paralegal

PAS/PAT/PATH (feeling, suffering, disease)
apathy
sympathy
empathy
antipathy

passionate
compassion
compatible
dispassionate
impassive
pathos
pathology
sociopath
psychopath

PATER/PATR (father, support)
patron
patronize
paternal
paternalism
expatriate
patrimony
patriarch
patrician

PO/POV/PAU/PU (few, little, poor)
poor
poverty
paucity
pauper
impoverish
puerile
pusillanimous

PED (child, education)
pedagogue
pediatrician
encyclopedia

PED/POD (foot)
pedal
pedestal
pedestrian

podiatrist
expedite
expedient
impede
impediment
podium
antipodes

PEN/PUN (to pay, to compensate)
penal
penalty
punitive
repent
penance
penitent
penitentiary
repine
impunity

PEND/PENS (to hang, to weigh, to pay)
depend
dispense
expend
stipend
spend
expenditure
suspense
compensate
propensity
pensive
indispensable
impending
pendulum
appendix
append
appendage
ponderous
pendant

PER (completely, wrong)
persistent
perforate
perplex
perspire
peruse
pervade
perjury
perturb
perfunctory
perspicacious
permeate
pernicious
perennial
peremptory
pertinacious

PERI (around)
perimeter
periscope
peripheral
peripatetic

PET/PIT (to go, to seek, to strive)
appetite
compete
petition
perpetual
impetuous
petulant
propitious

PHIL (love)
philosophy
philanthropy
philatelist
philology
bibliophile

PHONE (sound)
telephone
symphony
megaphone
euphony
cacophony

PLAC (to please)
placid
placebo
placate
implacable
complacent
complaisant

PLE (to fill)
complete
deplete
complement
supplement
implement
plethora
replete

PLEX/PLIC/PLY (to fold, to twist, to tangle, to bend)
complex
complexion
complicate
duplex
replica
ply
comply
implicit
implicate
explicit
duplicity
complicity
supplicate

accomplice
explicate

PON/POS/POUND (to put, to place)
component
compound
deposit
dispose
expose
exposition
expound
juxtapose
depose
proponent
repository
transpose
superimpose

PORT (to carry)
import
portable
porter
portfolio
deport
deportment
export
portmanteau
portly
purport
disport
importune

POST (after)
posthumous
posterior
posterity
ex post facto

PRE (before)
precarious
precocious
prelude
premeditate
premonition
presage
presentiment
presume
presuppose
precedent
precept
precipitous
preclude
predilection
preeminent
preempt
prepossess
prerequisite
prerogative

PREHEND/PRISE (to take, to get, to seize)
surprise
comprehend
enterprise
impregnable
reprehensible
apprehension
comprise
apprise
apprehend
comprehensive
reprisal

PRO (much, for, a lot)
prolific
profuse
propitious
prodigious

profligate
prodigal
protracted
proclivity
proliferate
propensity
prodigy
proselytize
propound
provident
prolix

PROB (to prove, to test)
probe
probation
approbation
probity
opprobrium
reprobate

PUG (to fight)
pugilism
pug
pugnacious
impugn
repugnant

PUNC/PUNG/POIGN/POINT (to point, to prick)
point
puncture
punctual
punctuate
pungent
poignant
compunction
expunge
punctilious

QUE/QUIS (to seek)
acquire
acquisition
exquisite
acquisitive
request
conquest
inquire
inquisitive
inquest
query
querulous
perquisite

QUI (quiet)
quiet
disquiet
tranquil
acquiesce
quiescent

RID/RIS (to laugh)
ridicule
derision
risible

ROG (to ask)
interrogate
arrogant
prerogative
abrogate
surrogate
derogatory
arrogate

SAL/SIL/SAULT/SULT (to leap, to jump)
insult
assault
somersault

salient
resilient
insolent
desultory
exult

SACR/SANCT/SECR (sacred)
sacred
sacrifice
sanctuary
sanctify
sanction
execrable
sacrament
sacrilege

SCI (to know)
science
conscious
conscience
unconscionable
omniscient
prescient
conscientious
nescient

SCRIBE/SCRIP (to write)
scribble
describe
script
postscript
prescribe
proscribe
ascribe
inscribe
conscription
scripture
transcript

circumscribe
manuscript
scribe

SE (apart)
select
separate
seduce
seclude
segregate
secede
sequester
sedition

SEC/SEQU (to follow)
second
prosecute
sequel
sequence
consequence
inconsequential
obsequious
non sequitur

SED/SESS/SID (to sit, to be still, to plan, to plot)
preside
resident
sediment
session
obsession
residual
sedate
subside
subsidy
subsidiary
sedentary
dissident
insidious

assiduous
sedulous

SENS/SENT (to feel, to be aware)
sense
sensual
sensory
sentiment
resent
consent
dissent
assent
consensus
sentinel
insensate
sentient
presentiment

SOL (to loosen, to free)
dissolve
soluble
solve
resolve
resolution
irresolute
solvent
dissolution
dissolute
absolution

SPEC/SPIC/SPIT (to look, to see)
perspective
aspect
spectator
specter
spectacles
speculation
suspicious

auspicious
spectrum
specimen
introspection
retrospective
perspicacious
circumspect
conspicuous
respite
specious

STA/STI (to stand, to be in a place)
static
stationary
destitute
obstinate
obstacle
stalwart
stagnant
steadfast
constitute
constant
stasis
status
status quo
homeostasis
apostasy

SUA (smooth)
suave
assuage
persuade
dissuade

SUB/SUP (below)
submissive
subsidiary
subjugate
subliminal

subdue
sublime
subtle
subversive
subterfuge
subordinate
suppress
supposition

SUPER/SUR (above)
surpass
supercilious
superstition
superfluous
superlative
supersede
superficial
surmount
surveillance
survey

TAC/TIC (to be silent)
reticent
tacit
taciturn

TAIN/TEN/TENT/TIN (to hold)
contain
detain
pertain
pertinacious
tenacious
abstention
sustain
tenure
pertinent
tenant
tenable

tenet
sustenance

TEND/TENS/TENT/TENU (to stretch, to thin)
tension
extend
tendency
tendon
tent
tentative
contend
contentious
tendentious
contention
contender
tenuous
distend
attenuate
extenuating

THEO (god)
atheist
apotheosis
theocracy
theology

TOM (to cut)
tome
microtome
epitome
dichotomy

TORT (to twist)
tort
extort
torture
tortuous

TRACT (to drag, to pull, to draw)
tractor
attract
contract
detract
tract
tractable
intractable
protract
abstract

TRANS (across)
transfer
transaction
transparent
transport
transition
transitory
transient
transgress
transcendent
intransigent
traduce
translucent

US/UT (to use)
abuse
usage
utensil
usurp
utility
utilitarian

VEN/VENT (to come, to move toward)
adventure
convene
convenient
event

venturesome
avenue
intervene
advent
contravene
circumvent

VER (truth)
verdict
verify
veracious
verisimilitude
aver
verity

VERS/VERT (to turn)
controversy
revert
subvert
invert
divert
diverse
aversion
extrovert
introvert
inadvertent
versatile
traverse
covert
overt
avert
advert

VI (life)
vivid
vicarious
convivial
viable
vivacity

joie de vivre
bon vivant

VID/VIS (to see)
evident
television
video
vision
provision
adviser
provident
survey
vista
visionary
visage

VOC/VOK (to call)
vocabulary
vocal
provocative

advocate
equivocate
equivocal
vocation
avocation
convoke
vociferous
irrevocable
evocative
revoke
invoke

VOL (to wish)
voluntary
volunteer
volition
malevolent
benevolent

Grammar and Usage

4

GRAMMAR. WHY LEARN IT?

Well, there's the mercenary reason: You need it to get good grades in school and to score well on exams such as the PSAT and the SAT II: Writing. But there's a better reason: self-expression. Understanding correct grammar and usage will enable you to say and write what you mean, clearly, concisely, and possibly elegantly.

THE PARTS OF SPEECH

The parts of speech are the roles that words play. You can write and speak beautiful English without knowing the *names* of these roles, but you do have to know how to use them correctly. And we can't teach you how to use them correctly if you don't know what they're called. So here they are—not every single one, but the ones you most need to know.

NOUN

A noun is a word that names something:

a person:	Gayle, Maria, student, guy
a place:	Korea, park, state, treetop
a thing:	horse, flower, money, Declaration of Independence
an idea:	truth, justice, the American way

Helpful Hint: Nouns are often preceded by *the*, *a*, or *an*.

In the following sentences, the **nouns** are in bold:

> Lying on his **back** in **bed,** he gazes around the **walls** of his **room**, musing about what has happened to his **collection** of **statements.** They had been discreetly mounted on **cardboard**, and fastened up with **push pins** so as not to deface the **walls.** Gone now. Probably tossed out with the **rest** of the **junk**—all those eight-by-ten **colorprints** of the **Cubs**, **White Sox**, and **Bears**, junior-high **mementos**. Too bad. It would be comforting to have **something** to look up to.
>
> —Judith Guest, *Ordinary People*

PRONOUN

A pronoun is a word that takes the place of a noun. It replaces a person, place, thing, or idea in a sentence.

Subject Pronouns	Object Pronouns
I	me
you	you
he/she/it	him/her/it
we	us
they	them
(who)	(whom)

Possessive Pronouns

my	mine
your	yours
his/her/its	his/hers/its
our	ours
their	theirs
(whose)	(whose)

The word that a pronoun replaces is called the *antecedent*.

Ira is preparing to teach **his** class.

(**His** refers to Ira. "Ira" is the antecedent.)

Don't eat the grapes until I've washed **them**.

(**Them** refers to the grapes. "Grapes" is the antecedent.)

ADJECTIVE

An adjective is a word that describes, or modifies, a noun:

Baggy jeans **Smelly** sneakers	Tells you something about the noun
My sandwich	Tells you whose sandwich it is
That dog	Tells you which dog it is

In the sentences below, the adjectives are in bold:

The building is **shabby,** and inside, the lobby is **hot** and **dark.** He glances at **his** watch; too **dark** in here to make out the numbers. The **crisp** and **sunny** day he has left outside has nearly blinded him.

—Judith Guest, *Ordinary People*

VERB

A verb is an action word, but it doesn't have to be Arnold Schwarzenegger action.

Verbs can express physical action:	**run, talk, kick**
They can express mental action:	**feel, think, consider**
Or, they can express a state of being:	**be, appear, seem**

In the sentences below, the verbs are in bold:

The dancer **tapped** a rhythm on the floor.

You **look** great!

She **remembers** third grade as if it **were** yesterday.

ADVERB

An adverb is a word that modifies verbs, adjectives, or other adverbs. Adverbs tend to tell where, when, and how.

coming **here**	Tells you *where* the person is coming
leaving **soon**	Tells you *when* the person is leaving
running **quickly**	Tells you *how* the person is running

In the sentences below, the adverbs are in bold:

He steps over to his desk, rummaging **fiercely** for a minute.

— Judith Guest, *Ordinary People*

(*How* is he rummaging? Fiercely.)

He is **suddenly** aware of the other people on the street.

—Judith Guest, *Ordinary People*

(*When* is he aware? Suddenly.)

PREPOSITION

A preposition shows the relationship between a noun or pronoun and another word in the sentence. The relationships are often about time, space, and direction.

Prepositions

across	from
above/below	to
before/after	at
over/under	in
with/without	on
between	by
through	for
into	of

Prepositional Phrase

A prepositional phrase is a preposition and its object (the noun it is relating to).

in a box	**In** is a preposition. **Box** is the object of the preposition.
with a fox	**With** is a preposition. **Fox** is the object of the preposition.
on a train	**On** is a preposition. **Train** is the object of the preposition.

In the sentences below, the prepositional phrases are in bold:

There is a sign **over the door**: NO LOITERING. The counterman/waiter keeps glancing over, getting ready to catch him **in the act**. He carefully folds his straw **into a small rectangle** and drops it **into his jacket**.

—Judith Guest, *Ordinary People*

CONJUNCTION

A conjunction joins words or groups of words in a sentence. *Coordinating* conjunctions connect equal parts of a sentence. They connect words to words, phrases to phrases, and clauses to clauses.

Coordinating Conjunctions

and	nor
but	so
or	yet
for	

In the following sentences, the conjunctions are in bold:

Tomoko **and** Jen wanted to go out. (connects word to word)

They didn't know if they should go to a big dance club **or** to a small jazz bar. ("or" connects phrase to phrase)

Jen wasn't twenty-one, **but** she thought she would get in anyway. ("but" connects clause to clause.)

Subordinating conjunctions connect dependent, or subordinate, clauses with the independent, or main, clause.

Subordinating Conjunctions

although	since
because	until
before	unless
if	when
just as	while

Before they went out, Jen tried to make herself look as old as possible. ("Before they went out" is a subordinate clause; it cannot stand alone.)

Tomoko thought they should go to a dance club, **because** the crowd would be younger. ("Because the crowd would be younger" is a subordinate clause.)

When they got there, the bouncer took one look at Jen and turned them away. ("When they got there" is a subordinate clause.)

INTERJECTION

Hey!

Not.

An interjection is an expression that shows a particular feeling, or shows emphasis. Interjections often interrupt or begin sentences.

Wow, that dog is ugly.

You got a paper cut on your tongue? **Ouch.**

THE SENTENCE

A sentence is a group of words that expresses a complete thought. It is made up of two basic parts: the subject and the predicate.

SUBJECT

The subject of the sentence is the noun or pronoun that performs the action in the sentence. To find the subject of a sentence, first find the verb and then ask yourself *who* or *what* is doing it.

PREDICATE

The predicate is the part of the sentence that isn't the subject. It contains the verb. A predicate can be simple or it can be extremely complicated. In the following sentences, the subject is **bold** and the predicate is *italic*.

Simple: **Jen** *loved dancing.*

Complicated: *Although she couldn't get into most dance clubs,* **Jen** *loved dancing to loud music and spent many afternoons in her living room with the stereo turned all the way up, pretending she was Madonna.*

PHRASE

A phrase is a group of words that works together in a sentence as a single part of speech. A phrase can work as a noun, a verb, an adjective, or an adverb. It is not a complete thought and cannot stand alone as a sentence because it lacks either a subject or a verb.

Look at these examples from the above sentence:

dancing to loud music (Tells us *what* Jen loved, so it is
working as a noun

in her living room   (Tells us *where* Jen *spent* many afternoons, so it is working as an adverb)

CLAUSE

A clause is a group of words that has a subject and a verb. Clauses that can stand alone are called *independent clauses*; if you took away the rest of the sentence, an independent clause would still make sense. Clauses that cannot stand alone are called *dependent clauses*; they need the rest of the sentence in order to make sense.

Dependent clause: Although she couldn't get into most dance clubs (This cannot stand alone as a sentence.)

Independent clause: Jen loved dancing to loud music and spent many afternoons in her living room with the stereo turned all the way up, pretending she was Madonna. (This is a complete sentence on its own.)

PUTTING IT ALL TOGETHER

Now that you know the names of the ingredients, you need to know how to combine them. In this section we explain the seven elements of usage most important for high school students:

Subject-verb agreement

Pronoun agreement

Pronoun case

Parallelism

Comparison

Modifiers

Tense

Though it may seem so, the rules below were not made up just to torture you. Rather, they exist to make your writing clear, logical, and possibly elegant.

SUBJECT-VERB AGREEMENT

The Big Subject-Verb Agreement Rule: Singular subjects take singular verbs, and plural subjects take plural verbs.

Singular	Plural
She sings.	They sing.
Glen is.	Stephen and Jed are.

Agreement can be trickier when the verb comes before the subject:

There **are** the **books** you lost. (The subject is "books," which is plural, so the verb, **are**, is also plural.)

There are several other ways in which agreement can get difficult. Following are some tips for constructing good sentences and spotting bad ones.

Tip #1

To identify the subject in a sentence, cross off distracting phrases.

Is this sentence correct or incorrect?

One of the athletes are giving an interview.

Answer: Incorrect. To identify the subject, you may need to cross off distracting phrases. *Of the athletes* is a prepositional phrase (see above for more on prepositional phrases). Cross it off and you're left with *One* as the subject.

One *are giving* an interview? No.

One *is giving* an interview. Yes.

So the correct sentence is this:

One of the athletes *is giving* an interview.

Tip #2

These words are considered singular subjects.

someone	everybody
anyone	nobody
everyone	one
no one	each

somebody	either
anybody	neither

Is this sentence correct or incorrect?

Neither of the star players want more money.

Answer: Incorrect. *Neither* is singular. *Of the star players* is a prepositional phrase, which you should cross off in order to find the subject. Because *neither* is a singular subject, you need a singular verb, *wants*. (Think "they *want*, he or she *wants*.")

So the correct sentence is this:

Neither of the star players *wants* more money.

Tip #3

Linking two singular subjects with "or" makes the subject singular. This is also true for the constructions *either /or* and *neither/nor*.

Is this sentence correct or incorrect?

Either the center or the forward have modeling contracts.

Answer: Incorrect. *The center* is a singular subject and *the forward* is a singular subject. Linking the two with the construction "either/ or" keeps the subject singular, so it needs a singular verb: "has." So the correct sentence is this:

Either the center or the forward *has* a modeling contract.

Tip #4

Collective nouns are singular. Collective nouns are tricky because they are one thing made up of many people or many things. Here are some examples:

the number	the group
the amount	the team
the audience	the company
the family	the government
	the United States (or any country)

Is this sentence correct or incorrect?

The forward's family come to all her games.

Answer: Incorrect. *The forward's family* is a singular subject, so it needs a singular verb: "comes." So the correct sentence is this:

The forward's family *comes* to all her games.

PRONOUN AGREEMENT

The Big Pronoun Agreement Rule: A pronoun must refer clearly to a specific noun (the antecedent). If that noun is singular, the pronoun must be singular; if the noun is plural, the pronoun must be plural.

Plural: *Bob and Harry* are eating *their* Doritos. (It would be **incorrect** to write: Bob and Harry are eating *his* Doritos. Whose Doritos? Bob's? Harry's? It's unclear. "Bob and Harry" creates a plural noun, which needs the plural pronoun, "their.")

Singular: *Harry* is eating *his* Doritos. (It would be **incorrect** to write: Harry is eating *their* Doritos. "Harry" is singular, so you must use the singular pronoun, "his.")

Tip #1

The same words that cause trouble in **Subject-Verb Agreement** cause trouble here: someone, anybody, everyone, no one, etc. These pronouns are *singular*.

Wrong: Someone didn't eat *their* Doritos.

Right: Someone didn't eat *her* Doritos.

or

Someone didn't eat *his* Doritos.

or

Someone didn't eat *his* or *her* Doritos.

You see the problem? We often have to say "his or her" or "he or she," and because it's awkward, we use "their" or "they" instead—which is tolerable in speech, but is *wrong* in writing. To avoid the awkwardness of "his or her," you may need to rewrite as follows:

There is still one bag of Doritos.

Tip #2

You must also make sure that it is obvious which noun your pronoun refers to. Is this sentence correct or incorrect?

> **Marty had told Michael where the party was, but he didn't know whether it started at eight or nine.**

Answer: Incorrect. *Who* didn't know what time the party started? Marty or Michael? We don't know. So the correct sentence is this:

> **Marty had told Michael where the party was, but *Michael* didn't know whether it started at eight or nine.**

PRONOUN CASE

Don't you have one? You don't? Then where do you keep your pronouns?

Pronoun case refers to the form of the pronoun needed in a sentence. There are three forms or cases, as shown on pages 88–89: Subjective, objective, and possessive.

> **The Big Pronoun Case Rule:** How do you know when to use *I* and when to use *me*? When to use *she* and when to use *her*? Subject pronouns are used to perform the action in a sentence. Object pronouns receive the action; they are the object of the action.

Morgan asked his mother for ten dollars, so *she* gave it to *him*.

She gave. "She" is performing the action, so you use the subject pronoun. "Him" is the object of the action. The money is given to *him*, so you use the object pronoun.

Tip #1

Subject pronouns follow the verb *to be.*

This is true no matter what form or tense the verb is in: am, is, are, was, were, will be, has been, have been, had been, etc.

If someone calls me and asks to speak to Gabrielle, I should respond thus:

> "This is *she*." (*she* follows *is*.)

If your father asks you who broke the remote control, the grammatically correct answer is this:

> "It was *I*." (*I* follows *was*)

Of course, you're not going to say that, but in formal writing that's what's correct.

Tip #2

Object pronouns follow prepositions.

Examples: go with *him,* the book by *her,* a picture of *him*

Take a look at these sentences.

I'm after *them.*

"After" is a preposition, so the pronoun following it must be in the objective case: *them,* not "they."

It's between *me* and *her.*

"Between" is a preposition, so the pronouns following it must be in the objective case: "me" and "her," not "I" and "she."

Tip #3

Cross out words that get in the way. Is this sentence correct or incorrect?

Roberto brought the books to Jin-hee and I.

Answer: Incorrect. Should you use *I* or *me*? Cross out "Jin-hee and" and listen to the sentence that way: "Roberto brought the books to I"? Now you can hear that that's wrong. So the correct sentence is this:

Roberto brought the books to Jin-hee and *me.*

Tip #4

When you are comparing two people in some way, use the subject pronoun. Is this sentence correct or incorrect?

Ira is better dressed than him.

Answer: Incorrect. When you make a comparison, what you are really saying is "Ira is better dressed than he *is.*" The "is" is implied. So the correct sentence is this:

Ira is better dressed than *he.*

Tip #5

Use the possessive pronoun with gerunds.

What's a gerund? A gerund is an *–ing* verb that functions as a noun.

> **Wrong:** Simon was upset about me leaving.

> **Right:** Simon was upset about *my* leaving.

What was Simon upset about? The leaving. *My* leaving. He wasn't upset about *me*, he was upset about my *leaving*.

Tip #6

Who is a subject and *whom* is an object. Use *who* if you would use *he*; use *whom* if you would use *him*.

> The actor, about *whom* there had been endless gossip, finally gave an interview.

Would you say "about *he*" or "about *him*"? "About *him*," so you use *whom*.

> Who is coming tonight?

Would you say *"He* is coming tonight" or *"Him* is coming tonight"? *"He,"* so you use *who*.

PARALLELISM

> *Let every nation know, whether it wishes us well or ill, that we shall pay any price, bear any burden, meet any hardship, support any friend, oppose any foe to assure the survival and the success of liberty.*

> —John F. Kennedy

The Big Parallelism Rule: Ideas or actions in a series should be parallel in form.

Parallelism gives your writing elegance and clarity simply by maintaining consistency.

Example 1

> **Wrong:** The enclosed resume indicates that I am interested in writing, editing, and *I like to read*.

And you won't get the job. You are listing three things that you are interested in; the first two are nouns, so the third one must be a noun.

Right: The enclosed resume indicates that I am interested in writing, editing, and *reading*.

Example 2

When you use correlative conjunctions, which are two-part constructions such as *either/or, both/and,* and *not only/but also,* you must make the two parts match.

> **Wrong:** Allison works *both* **as a** massage therapist *and* **she is an** illustrator.

You are using the construction *both/and,* so what follows these two parts must match. "As a" and "she is an" do not match.

> **Right:** Allison works *both* **as a** massage therapist *and* **as an** illustrator.

COMPARISON

> *Power in defense of freedom is greater than power in behalf of tyranny and oppression.*
>
> —Malcolm X

Malcolm X was comparing two kinds of power. One kind of *power* is greater than another kind of *power*. The two things being compared are comparable.

The First Big Comparison Rule: When comparing actions, be sure to include both verbs. Is this sentence correct or incorrect?

Andra likes ice cream more than Randy.

Answer: Incorrect. Does Andra like ice cream more than Randy does? Or does Andra like ice cream *more than she likes Randy*? Does Randy know? Is Andra's passion for ice cream going to end the relationship? How can we end the suspense? The correct sentence is this:

Andra likes ice cream more than Randy *does*.

Oh. Don't compare *ice cream* to *Randy*. It causes problems.

The Second Big Comparison Rule: When comparing nouns, be sure both nouns are there and that they are comparable.

Is this sentence correct or incorrect?

A biography of Thoreau would be more interesting than Hawthorne.

Answer: Incorrect. You can't compare a biography to a man. You have to compare a biography to another biography (or at least another book). So the correct sentence is this:

A biography of Thoreau would be more interesting than *a biography of* **Hawthorne.**

MODIFIERS

The Big Modifier Rule: Put modifying phrases next to their subjects.

Is this sentence correct or incorrect?

Riding my bicycle, my pants got caught in the chain.

Answer: Incorrect. (Those must be some pants if they know how to ride a bicycle.) *Riding my bicycle* is a modifying phrase, i.e, it is describing something. What is it describing? It is supposed to be describing *I*, the person riding the bicycle; but because it is next to *my pants,* that's what it ends up describing. You can fix it by putting the subject next to the phrase. So the correct sentence is this:

Riding my bicycle, *I* **got my pants caught in the chain.**

Or you can add the subject to the modifying phrase. Another correct version is this:

As *I* **was riding my bicycle, my pants got caught in the chain.**

TENSE

The five simplest tenses are the following:

present:	I eat	*present perfect:*	I have eaten
past:	I ate	*past perfect:*	I had eaten
future:	I will eat		

Present

The present tense is used in three ways.

1. Statements of fact: The earth *revolves* around the sun.

2. Statements of habit: I *go* to school at seven-thirty every day.

3. Some statements about right now: I *am* hungry.

Future

The future tense is used for things that will happen in the—guess what—future.

> They *will arrive* on Thursday.

THE PRESENT PERFECT, THE PAST, AND THE PAST PERFECT

These three tenses are often misused. The correct usage for each is explained below.

Present Perfect

The present perfect tense does not refer to a specific time. Use the present perfect to show the recent past and to show actions that started in the past and continue into the present. For example, if you say

> I *have braided* my hair.

you may be implying that your hair is still braided.

Past

Use the past tense if the action happened in the past and did not continue into the present. For example, if you say

> I *braided* my hair.

you could logically follow it with "Then I unbraided it."

Past Perfect

The past perfect tense shows that something took place *even before* something else in the past. Use it to make clear that one action happened before another, in the past. For example,

> I only realized how wet my hair still was after I *had braided* it.

Had braided shows that this had happened earlier than *realized*.

Sequence of Tenses

Certain tenses can correctly be used together, as in the following examples.

> If I *had* a hammer, I *would hammer* in the morning.

> If I *were* a rich man, all day long I *would* biddy-biddy-bum.

If I *go* to the party, I *will see* Janeane Garofalo.

If I *went* to the party, I *would see* Janeane Garofalo.

If I *had gone* to the party, I *would have seen* Janeane Garofalo.

Don't mix and match these. "If I *go* to the party, I *would see* Janeane Garofalo" is wrong.

SAY WHAT YOU MEAN

The following is a list of words that are commonly confused and misused. Be sure you know the differences between (or among) them. We give a sentence for each that should clarify the issue for you.

accept/except

I *accept* your challenge.

Everyone was able to go *except* me.

affect/effect

The movie *affected* me greatly.

The *effect* of all that beautiful music was inspiring.

allusion/illusion

The paper was filled with literary *allusions*.

I have no *illusion* that Professor Harper will pass me this term.

alternate/alternative

Marie *alternated* shifts with Paolo; every other week, she took evenings and he took days.

There are only a few *alternatives* to meat that are as high in protein.

ambiguous/ambivalent

Professor Smith warned us to be clear, not *ambiguous*, in the statement of our theses.

I'm still feeling *ambivalent* about whether to write about Monet or Manet.

between/among

Between the two of us, Mary is the stronger.

Among the students in the class, Roger is the smartest.

bring/take

Bring the book to me.

Take the book away.

can/may

I *can* finally swim! Mary taught me.

May I go to the party with you?

censor/censure

The panel *censored* the movie by removing all objectionable material before it was released.

The student board decided to *censure* the student for cheating on an exam.

common/mutual

We have a *common* purpose. (meaning *shared purpose*)

We have a *mutual* attraction. (meaning a *reciprocal attraction*)

compliment/complement

Dean Smith *complimented* my ability to get to class on time.

Mashed potatoes are the perfect *complement* to roast beef.

continual/continuous

The students formed a *continuous* line that surrounded the building to protest its demolition.

The program was interrupted every few minutes by a *continual* banging in the pipes.

emigrate/immigrate

People *emigrated* from Ireland to the United States.

They *immigrated* to our country to escape great famine in their own.

eminent/immanent/imminent

The author is the *eminent* source in the field of physics.

The *immanent* faith of St. Theresa of Avila is what makes her so appealing.

The due date for that paper is *imminent*.

farther/further

Florida is *farther* from here than Maryland is.

I hope to *further* my discussion of Kierkegaard in the next paper I write.

fewer/less

We ordered *fewer* sheets of paper from the store this time.

I have *less* work to do.

former/latter

I have two classes on Tuesday: biology and aerobics. The *former* is in the science building, but the *latter* is in the field house.

fortuitous/fortunate

It was *fortuitous* to find that book on the shelf—it was exactly what I needed.

I was *fortunate* to get into the intro art history class—it's almost always full.

healthy/healthful

I hope to eat a *healthful* diet while away at school.

Marina always works better when she is *healthy*.

implicit/explicit

The tone of his voice made it *implicit* to the class that poor work would not be tolerated.

Professor Jones *explicitly* stated that we were not to write one word over three pages for that assignment.

incredible/incredulous

It was an *incredible* sight: an ape rescuing a small child.

The crowd was *incredulous*: They were sure the ape would harm the child.

infer/imply

Gene *inferred* that Marta was a pretty tactless person.

Marta *implied* that Gene had gained weight when she asked him if those pants were tight.

its/it's

A dog likes to have a place to call *its* own: a pillow, dog bed, or corner.

It's important to feed your pet every day.

libel/slander

Roseanne was foolish not to sue that tabloid for *libel* when they printed that story about her.

The speaker *slandered* several of her colleagues that night when she gave a scathing indictment of the new departmental policy.

lie/lay

I need to *lie* down after that crazy day.

I *lay* the book down in the hallway.

most/more

Of the ten books we read for our literature class, I enjoyed *Jane Eyre* the *most*.

Of the two books I read this week, I enjoyed *Jane Eyre* *more*.

respectfully/respectively

Ginger had been taught to bow *respectfully* when her elders entered the room.

I hope to meet with Jim and John, *respectively*, to iron out this problem.

their/they're/there

> We want to meet Milo and Otto after class in *their* dorm room.

> *They're* not going to be happy that we are there.

> *There* is a way to find the answer to your problem.

your/you're

> This is *your* paper, so write it from *your* perspective.

> If *you're* going to write this paper, you should do a good job.

5

A Selective Timeline of British Literature

Timelines serve one purpose: They show information *at a glance*. If you can never remember whether Wordsworth was a Romantic, or Pope a satirist—if you don't know your Rationalism from your Modernism, your Regency from your Renaissance—a timeline is what you need. In the following pages you'll find the basics: writers, what they wrote, and what was going on (politically, economically, etc.), while they were writing. There are no lengthy expositions of particular works, nor are there any tips on how to read the authors in the timeline—just a simple chronology of who was doing what and when they were doing it.

When referring to this chapter, there are one or two things to keep in mind. First, this is a *selective* timeline. It is by no means exhaustive as a list of writers or their works. It focuses on writers and works you're likely to encounter (or at least hear of) in high school or college. So don't come away with the idea that Milton, for example, *only* wrote *Paradise Lost* and *Paradise Regained,* or that Swift *only* wrote *Gulliver's Travels,* or that there were no other writers of any significance or merit between George Orwell and Samuel Beckett. Remember, it's a rough guide.

Second, it's important to realize that historical periods don't generally begin and end abruptly. In this timeline, for example, you'll see the Age of Reason (1660–1800) followed by the Romantic Period (1798–1832). Don't get hung up on the dividing lines between the periods. They are approximate. Rationalist satirism did not die in 1798—there are writers in this genre even today.

Finally, you'll see that Homer has been included in the British literature timeline, which is completely inaccurate, because Homer (if he existed at all, about which there is still much debate) was Greek. The reason for his inclusion is that *The Iliad* and *The Odyssey* have had a tremendous influence on English language literature. There are so many references to these two works in the succeeding entries of the timeline that to leave them out of the picture would be to handicap students hopelessly.

**Homer
(Greek, circa 700
B.C.E.)**
The Iliad
The Odyssey

THE ANGLO-SAXONS
(449–1066)

Beowulf, the first great work of English literature, was written sometime around 700 C.E., almost a century before the Vikings invaded England. *Beowulf* was written in the time during which the Angles and the Saxons, peoples originally from Germany, ruled England. (Where does the name "England" come from? The rule of the Angles led to the country being called "Engla land," and eventually "England").

As is reflected in *Beowulf*, the story of a man's effort to save his king from a monster, Anglo-Saxon society focused on loyalty to one's leader. The leader was responsible for law and order, but communal decision-making was common. Anglo-Saxons were fighters who spent a lot of time defending their families and territory, and many of them worshiped warrior gods. Despite their military culture, the Anglo-Saxons were ahead of their time with women's rights: Women were allowed to inherit property and got to keep it even when they got married.

THE MIDDLE AGES (1066–1485)

This was the era of knights, chivalry, and castles. You may have seen Hollywood's version in one of those Richard Burton films on late night TV in which all the men were dressed up as priests, kings, or knights and wearing a lot of heavy gold jewelry. Much of the death-defying drama portrayed in these movies is based in reality and had a lot to do with the social structure at the time, known as *feudalism*.

The Middle Ages began when Duke William (also known as William the Conqueror) of Normandy, a region in what we now know as France, crossed the channel and successfully invaded England in 1066. Known as the Norman Conquest, Duke William's takeover changed a lot of things for England. England became more like the rest of feudalist Europe. Under feudalism, a very powerful person, like a king, would allot some of his land to a small group of powerful people, called barons, in return for economic or military allegiance. The barons would then divide up their land and make the same arrangement with other well-off people, and so on. These wealthy landowners lived in castles, with poor people, or serfs, as their slaves, and they needed knights to defend their property. Boys who were not born as serfs were taken from their homes and trained to be knights. (Although you got to be called "sir" when you were a knight, life wasn't always that great: The 120-pound armor they wore was so hot and heavy that some of them died from heatstroke.) Meanwhile, women had no political rights and were ruled by their husbands, fathers, or brothers.

**Geoffrey Chaucer
(1343–1400)**
The Canterbury Tales

As the population of England grew, people started moving to towns and cities, which freed them of the landowners, or "overlords." The characters of **Geoffrey Chaucer**, author of the *Canterbury Tales*, were often living in towns or villages. Meanwhile, England and the rest of Europe were going through some bigger changes. Although Europeans had set off to convert the Muslims of the Middle East to Christianity (a series of invasions called the *Crusades*), they discovered that their own way of life was a bit lacking. The crusaders brought back new ideas about architecture, math, and astronomy from the people of the Middle East. In 1215, an event with enormous political ramifications took place in England: King John was forced by a group of barons to sign a document called the Magna Carta. The Magna Carta limited the power of the king, and of the Pope, granting certain rights to the barons and even to other subjects. This document later became the basis for English constitutional law.

Papal control and feudalism were further weakened after what is called England's "Hundred Years' War" (1337–1453) with France. Small landowners were important to the war effort and became more powerful. Finally, the spread of the bubonic plague, or the Black Death, which hit England in 1348–49, dealt a fatal blow to feudalism. So many people died that there was a labor shortage, and any time there's a labor shortage, poor people become more powerful. The serfs were becoming free at last.

THE RENAISSANCE (1485–1660)

The word *renaissance* is French for "rebirth"—and that's exactly what was happening, intellectually, artistically, and politically, in England and throughout Europe.

Much of the developments of this period were the result of people studying Greek and Latin and discovering the power of literary and scholarly works from ancient Rome and Greece. With the recent invention of the printing press, books were available to many more people. (Before the printing press, every book was written out *by hand*.) This flood of new ideas and information made Europeans increasingly curious about the world and stimulated developments in philosophy and the arts. The discoveries and artistic achievements of this era shaped today's world: In 1492 Christopher Columbus set sail; in 1503 Leonardo da Vinci painted the Mona Lisa; in 1543 Copernicus theorized that planets orbit the sun; and in 1609 Galileo was the first to use a

William Shakespeare (1564–1616)
Plays including:
Hamlet
Macbeth
King Lear
Romeo and Juliet
A Midsummer Night's Dream
The Tempest
Poems

John Milton (1608–1674)
Paradise Lost
Paradise Regained

WILLIAM SHAKESPEARE (1564–1616)

Kings, beggars, heroes, villains, temptresses, hypocrites, jesters, politicians, and serving wenches—Shakespeare created dramatic representations of them all. His ability to portray the human character in all its shades of vice and virtue is unsurpassed, and he pulled it off in some of the most beautiful language the English-speaking world has ever known. It seems as if all he had to do was reach out toward a character, give her a couple of lines of dialogue, and bam! the character lived, completely.

One of the reasons Shakespeare wrote so many and such varied plays was that he was working furiously to meet the demands of his adoring public. From his mid-twenties on, Shakespeare worked as both an actor and a playwright for a theatrical company in London. His plays were huge successes, and between 1592 and 1607 he wrote at least one, and often two, per year, with the plays being performed by his company as quickly as he could produce them.

Shakespeare was popular with everyone in his audience, from those who paid a penny for general admission to Queen Elizabeth and her successor King James. Shakespeare had become a shareholder in his theatrical company, and the success of his plays eventually brought him significant wealth. He used some of his profits to help finance the construction of the famous Globe theater.

telescope. In the late 1580s **William Shakespeare** began to write for the stage. The Roman Catholic Church, which had grown very wealthy due to its control over most of Great Britain and Europe, funded many of the Renaissance scholars, artists, and architects.

While all of this was happening, some people began thinking more about what it means to be a human being and how to live a fulfilling life. They became part of an intellectual movement known today as *humanism*. They talked about personal freedom and questioned whether the purpose of life was to become as rich and powerful as possible or to be a moral person. At the same time, the authority of the Roman Catholic Church was being challenged all over Europe. Many people began to resent the Pope's control over their lives and began to think about religion in new ways. Those who broke with the Roman Catholic Church and began different Christian religions were part of the movement called the *Reformation*. Lutherans, Baptists, Presbyterians, and members of other Protestant denominations can trace their history back to this time. In England, King Henry VIII's anger at the Pope for refusing to grant him a divorce (so that he could marry another woman—Anne Boleyn—whom he later beheaded) led him to start his own church, called the Church of England.

When Henry's daughter Elizabeth became queen, she was much more popular than Henry had been. She was a successful law-and-order kind of ruler who brought peace to England and believed in its independence. Many writers and poets of the day wrote about Elizabeth or dedicated their work to her, and the time of her rule has come to be referred to as the Elizabethan period.

THE AGE OF REASON
(1660–1800)

Compared to all the fighting about religion during the Renaissance, the eighteenth century was a pretty calm time. England had amassed quite an empire around the world, with colonies in the Americas made lucrative by the labor of enslaved Africans. Although the American Revolution ended England's control over the North American colonies, England remained one of the world's major powers. The country's educated and wealthy elite were free to spend a lot of their time reading, writing, and socializing. If you were rich, you probably had read the Latin classics in school. If you were a writer, you probably tried to imitate the way they wrote in ancient Rome. You were also, undoubtedly, quite taken with the new scientific discoveries of the time. The reason that the eighteenth century is dubbed the *Age of Reason* or the *Enlightenment* is because people became increasingly interested in figuring out, logically, how the universe worked. They wanted rational, not merely religious, explanations for natural phenomena like comets, lightning, and snowstorms.

While members of the growing middle class were busy looking at the stars, England's poor were living in tiny, windowless, rat-infested cellars. The gap between rich and poor during this era began to grow. Many people, particularly children, died of smallpox and other poverty-related diseases. The developments in science hadn't yet improved medical knowledge much, but even if they had, most doctors would only treat the wealthy. The "immorality" and lavish lifestyles of the eighteenth century's rich and famous were the targets of poets and essayists like **Alexander Pope** and **Jonathan Swift**, who were masters at satire. Eventually the reading public

**Aphra Behn
(1640–1689)**
Oroonoko, or the History of the Royal Slave

**Daniel Defoe
(1660–1731)**
*Robinson Crusoe
Moll Flanders
Roxanna*

**Jonathan Swift
(1667–1745)**
Gulliver's Travels

**Alexander Pope
(1688–1744)**
The Rape of the Lock

**Henry Fielding
(1707–1754)**
Tom Jones

JANE AUSTEN (1775–1817)

"that exquisite touch which renders ordinary common-place things and characteristics interesting"

—Sir Walter Scott

Scott's words are true of many writers, but especially so of Jane Austen, whose fiction is typically set within the narrow parameters of the eighteenth-century drawing room. Her observations on class, love, morality, power, and human vices and virtues are all brilliantly teased out in novels in which the characters rarely do anything more dramatic than go for a walk in the garden or pour the tea. Given her background, this isn't surprising: A clergyman's daughter born in 1775, the second youngest of seven children, Austen spent the bulk of her life with her comfortable and affectionate family. She also never married—strange, perhaps, given that the problem of finding suitable husbands for eligible daughters is a recurring theme in her novels. Austen's writing is characterized by delicate wit, rich irony, and cutting satire. Her language is cool and polished, and none of the objects of her ridicule is ever handled viciously. As a whole, her work offers a unique, intelligent woman's perspective on the manners and morals of her time, along with poignant insights into human character that still resonate for twentieth-century readers.

Jane Austen
(1775–1817)
Pride and Prejudice
Emma
Sense and Sensibility

William Blake
(1757–1827)
Poems and Prose
Songs of Innocence and Experience

William Wordsworth
(1770–1850)
Poems

wanted longer reads, and the first novels were published by writers **Henry Fielding** and **Aphra Behn**, who wrote an early anti-slavery novel. The field of journalism developed during this era as well, with newspapers offering ever more opportunities for social commentary.

THE ROMANTIC PERIOD (1798–1832)

The name conjures up sunsets and lovers holding hands, but for an accurate picture think overcrowded cities, child labor, soot and smoke in the air. This was the era in which the **Industrial Revolution** really took hold. England's agriculture-based economy was on its way out. People were beginning to move from farms to cities and mill towns to find work. Many ended up in disease-ridden slums. But the government, adopting a new theory called *laissez faire* economics, rejected any responsibility for the people's poverty by saying that the economy should be free of governmental interference.

This was also a time of war. In 1789, the French stormed the Bastille prison, revolting against King Louis XVI in the name of a more democratic society. The **French Revolution** sent shock waves throughout England and Europe. The wealthy supporters of the monarchy in England, who were afraid that the disenfranchised English masses might get the same idea, started cracking down on any dissent. In 1805, England went to war against France, which was then controlled by Napoleon Bonaparte, who—to the dismay of many of the revolution's supporters—became as brutal a ruler as the beheaded king had been.

All of this was pretty depressing to liberal English intellectuals and writers, who had hoped that the French Revolution might spark real social change in England. Much of the best literature of the time reflects the idealistic, or romantic, views of the writers who envisioned a better world. As an antidote of sorts to the new city-bound life of many working people, poets like **William Wordsworth, Samuel Taylor Coleridge**, and **William Blake** wrote frequently of their passionate love of nature and their belief in the supremacy of the laws of the natural world. Within

Samuel Taylor Coleridge (1772–1834)
Poems, including "The Rime of the Ancient Mariner"

Lord Byron (1778–1824)
Poems

Percy Bysshe Shelly (1792–1822)
Poems

John Keats (1795–1821)
Poems

Mary Wollstonecraft Shelly (1797–1851)
Frankenstein, or the Modern Prometheus

JOHN KEATS (1795–1821)

In many ways, Keats is *the* Romantic poet: huge appetite for life, deeply affected by the natural world, passionately in love—and tragically afflicted with tuberculosis, which killed him when he was only 25 years old. Keats is the James Dean of poetry; his short, intense life has become (like Dean's) an icon of doomed youth. He's also the guy responsible for the now immortal line, "Beauty is truth, truth beauty—that is all / Ye know on earth, and all ye need to know," the exact meaning of which critics have been arguing about ever since it was written. His poetry is like a nuclear assault on all five senses, using language that focuses on textures, tastes, sounds, smells, and images. Keats knew his health was fragile, and so worked furiously to hone his "poetical talent" while he could. He was capable of producing a masterpiece in just a few hours, once saying, "if poetry does not come as naturally as the leaves to a tree, it had better not come at all."

the spirit of the times, the form of poetry was itself revolutionized—the writing was no longer as formal and witty as that of the Eighteenth century, but was becoming more simple, emotional, and imaginative. Poets began to see themselves not just as entertainers or commentators, but teachers, and their poems as sources of inspiration for all people.

Elizabeth Barrett Browning (1806–1861)
Sonnets from the Portuguese
Aurora Leigh

Alfred, Lord Tennyson (1809–1892)
Poems

THE VICTORIAN PERIOD (1832–1901)

In this era Great Britain began to consider the consequences of becoming the world's first industrialized nation. After Napoleon was defeated at the battle of Waterloo in 1815, England experienced a long period of peace under the reign of Queen Victoria. The English began to examine their society more closely, considering

CHARLOTTE AND EMILY BRONTË (1816–1855, 1818–1848)

Charlotte Brontë

Emily Brontë

The Victorian age was a chauvinistic one, which is why Charlotte and Emily—and the somewhat less famous Anne—published their work under the male pseudonyms Currer, Ellis, and Acton Bell. Where did the Brontë sisters get their material? It's a mystery. For women who grew up in an isolated parsonage on England's Yorkshire moors, they seemed awfully familiar with grand passions and wild times. It's no surprise that Charlotte thought Jane Austen limited. Charlotte's best novel, *Jane Eyre*, is anything but the stuff of provincial drawing rooms. Her heroine is a governess who is cool, rational, and a model of propriety on the surface. Beneath the surface, however, Jane Eyre is passionate, imaginative, and profoundly affected by elemental forces of nature. She falls for the brooding Mr. Rochester, who, among his other shortcomings, has a mad wife locked away in his attic.

Emily's only novel, *Wuthering Heights,* is regarded by some as one of the greatest novels in the English language. Why? Well, for one thing, it contains Heathcliff—a romantic character who's so wrecked by his memory of lost love that he'd set his dogs on you at the drop of a hat. Whereas the protagonists usually struggle between Reason and Passion in Charlotte's novels, in Emily's *Wuthering Heights* Passion rules virtually unchallenged. If you want to know what a *genuinely* Romantic novel feels like, read this one.

GEORGE ELIOT (1819–1880)

George Eliot was the pen name of Mary Ann Evans, who, like the Brontë sisters, initially chose to conceal her gender behind a male pseudonym. Highly intelligent, serious, and never afraid of large themes, Eliot had the ability to portray the same event from multiple fictional viewpoints, with all the moral relativity that implied. She defied Victorian convention (albeit anxiously) by "living in sin" with G. H. Lewes (who was already married to someone else), a relationship that lasted until Lewes died in 1878. Her most famous work, *Middlemarch*, published 1871–72, deals with, among other things, the predicament of the intelligent, idealistic woman struggling to find meaningful expression in a community where the options are claustrophobically traditional. With the publication of this novel, Eliot reached the height of her fame, and was widely regarded as the greatest living English novelist, with fans including Henry James and Queen Victoria.

both the changes brought by the Industrial Revolution—the creation of new towns and cities, more affordable goods and services—and the absence of political change that many thought necessary. There was growing dissatisfaction with the government, particularly in the wake of a major economic depression in the 1840s and the influx of refugees from Ireland due to famine there. (Much of the hunger was caused by damage to Ireland's major crop, potatoes, which is why the time is known as the Irish Potato Famine.)

So while many English were proud of the technological and material progress that the country had made, others focused on the desperate need for societal reform. These "reformers," or political activists, worked toward higher public health standards, better housing conditions, and limits on child labor. The first public schools were opened in 1870. Many more people learned to read and libraries were established. Meanwhile, after years of widespread political demonstrations, most men won the right to vote during this era. Women, however, wouldn't be allowed to vote until the next century.

The people of the Victorian era had strong

Robert Browning (1812–1889)
Poems

Charles Dickens (1812–1870)
David Copperfield
A Tale of Two Cities
Bleak House
Great Expectations
Hard Times
Nicholas Nickleby

Charlotte Brontë (1816–1855)
Jane Eyre

Emily Brontë (1818–1848)
Wuthering Heights

George Eliot [Mary Ann Evans] (1819–1880)
Middlemarch

OSCAR WILDE (1854–1900)

Read Oscar Wilde. You'll like him. Wit didn't start with him, but he took it a long way. A dramatist, poet, and novelist, whose specialty was providing a snappy answer to any stupid question, Wilde's work is chiefly characterized by brilliant aphorisms, epigrams, and social observations on class, morality, and manners. He was a champion of the "art for art's sake" philosophy, which means, roughly, that the aesthetic (or beauty) operates independently of any other consideration: "There is no such thing as a moral or an immoral book. Books are well written or badly written. That is all."

Being gay in the latter part of the Nineteenth century wasn't easy—and for someone as outspoken and luminous as Wilde, it was almost sure to bring trouble. After a court battle with the marquess of Queensbury, over his involvement with her son, Wilde was imprisoned for homosexual "offenses" in 1895. He served two years, went bankrupt, moved to France, and died in Paris in 1900.

His best works are the plays *Lady Windemere's Fan, An Ideal Husband, A Woman of No Importance,* and (his masterpiece) *The Importance of Being Earnest.*

Lewis Carroll [Charles Lutwidge Dodgson] (1832–1898)
Alice's Adventures in Wonderland
Through the Looking Glass

Thomas Hardy (1840–1928)
Tess of the D'Urbervilles
Jude the Obscure
Far From the Madding Crowd
The Return of the Native

Robert Louis Stevenson (1850–1894)
Treasure Island
The Strange Case of Dr. Jekyll and Mr. Hyde

Oscar Wilde (1854–1900)
The Importance of Being Earnest

The people of the Victorian era had strong ideas about what kind of behavior, ideas, and art were acceptable. The magazines and books of the time generally would not allow any mention of sex; health care workers were even arrested for distributing information about sexually transmitted diseases. The social codes of the day were particularly hard on women. Women were judged much more harshly then men for failing to do what society expected. In her poetic novel, *Aurora Leigh,* **Elizabeth Barrett Browning** criticized society's treatment of women. Other Victorian writers used their poems, stories, and essays to question or make fun of the strictness of Victorian life. They also questioned whether material "progress" meant that life was getting better or worse. **Charles Dickens**, for example, created the character of Scrooge in *A Christmas Carol* as a way of raising the issue of whether wealth really brought true happiness.

THE TWENTIETH CENTURY

In the early part of this century the British Empire came to an end, while a dramatically new era in politics, science, philosophy, psychology, and literature began. The groundwork for some of these changes had been laid during the Victorian era by scholars like Charles Darwin, who, in 1859, had offered a theory of evolution that challenged the biblical account of creation. By the early 1900s, Victorian values of "morality" and stability were giving way to a new interest in questioning authority, order, and tradition. World War I, known then as the "Great War," profoundly changed the way that the English thought about their country. Along with France and Russia, England entered the war against Germany and what was then known as Austria-Hungary in 1914. Initially, young men in Great Britain jumped at the chance to defend their country; many rushed to enlist in the army. But by the end of the war in 1918—most of it fought from cold, filthy trenches in France—the attitude toward the war had changed. Almost 1 million

George Bernard Shaw (1856–1950)
Pygmalion

Joseph Conrad (1857–1924)
Heart of Darkness

William Butler Yeats (1865–1939)
Poems

Virginia Woolf (1882–1941)
Mrs. Dalloway
To The Lighthouse
A Room of One's Own

James Joyce (1882–1941)
Ulysses
A Portrait of the Artist as a Young Man
Dubliners
Finnegan's Wake

VIRGINIA WOOLF (1882–1941)

Modernist heavyweight and crucial member of "The Bloomsbury Group," a group of writers that hung out at 46 Gordon Square, Bloomsbury, London, united in (an arguably elitist) revolt against artistic, sexual, and social restrictions of their day. Don't be fooled by that word "revolt," by the way; it's not like they were out wrecking public monuments. Woolf wrote one of the classics of feminism, the essay *A Room of One's Own*, in which she argued that a woman would not be able to fulfill her potential without the privacy and independence implied by the title.

Low on plot, high on experiment and innovation, Woolf's best known novels, *Jacob's Room, Mrs. Dalloway*, and *To the Lighthouse*, show her moving beyond the traditional modes of characterization by focusing on the complexities of experience. Like Joyce, she used interior monologue and stream-of-consciousness techniques to make fiction more like internal experience. Brainy, sensitive, and highly attuned to the subtleties of human consciousness, Woolf made a tremendous impact on fiction; many of the narrative techniques she developed are now standard, and her penetrating examination of the conflict between the principle male and female characters (see especially *To the Lighthouse*) remains strikingly insightful, and is relevant to present-day readers.

D. H. LAWRENCE (1885–1930)

Renowned for having written the formerly banned *Lady Chatterly's Lover* (a sad fact, because it's one of the weakest novels he wrote), Lawrence's contribution to English fiction is a mighty one. His father was a coal miner, his mother an ex-schoolteacher—a disastrous British class combination Lawrence depicts in *Sons and Lovers*, one of the grittiest, most moving novels ever set in a working class background.

Like Keats, Lawrence lived fast and died young—in his mid-forties—of tuberculosis. When he was 27, he met, fell in love with, and eloped with Frieda Weekly, the wife of one of his old professors. They remained together (in one of the stormiest relationships ever) thereafter, wandering from country to country, always short of cash, while Lawrence produced an incredible volume of letters, poems, essays, travel sketches, and novels right up to his death in 1930.

His most important novels are *The Rainbow* and its sequel, *Women in Love*. If you're looking for a single word to sum up Lawrence's writing, try "intense." He deals with the extremities and depths of human feeling in language that's passionate and highly poetic. Big themes are the order of the day: love, sex, power, politics, and religion.

D. H. Lawrence (1885–1930)
Sons and Lovers
The Rainbow
Women in Love
Lady Chatterly's Lover

Agatha Christie (1891–1976)
Murder on the Orient Express

Aldous Huxley (1894–1963)
Brave New World

George Orwell [Eric Blair] (1903–1950)
1984
Animal Farm
Collected Essays
Down and Out in Paris and London

British soldiers had died. Much of the public had lost its faith in the government and no longer believed in the "glory" of war or their country. Meanwhile, the late nineteenth century writings of German philosopher Karl Marx, who had envisioned an egalitarian economic system that would eliminate the extremes of wealth and poverty under capitalism, led to the Russian Revolution in 1917.

At the same time that traditional ideas about politics and patriotism were being called into question, conventional thinking about art and literature was challenged. Writers like **Virginia Woolf** and Ireland's **James Joyce** offered radically new ways of portraying human consciousness in their writing, redefining the novel. Other authors, such as **D. H. Lawrence**, wrote a number of controversial works that dealt with the reality of class conflict, sex, and relationships between women and men. The literature of the time was also influenced by Sigmund Freud, whose study of people's dreams led to his landmark theory that the key to understanding human behavior lies in the unconscious, the irrational, hidden part of our minds.

Soon, however, the world was heading for another war. A global economic depression—sparked by the U.S. stock market crash in 1929—made it easier for dictators like Germany's Adolph Hitler and Italy's Benito Mussolini to win the support of people who were desperate for stability and prosperity. When World War II broke out, England, under the leadership of Winston Churchill, fought against an invasion by Hitler's Nazi forces. During the war, Hitler succeeded in systematically murdering more than 6 million Jews in German-occupied countries in what is known as the Holocaust, as well as Gypsies, the disabled, homosexuals, Communists, and many other "undesirable" groups. The war ended on August 6, 1945, when the United States dropped an atomic bomb on Hiroshima, a city in Japan, which was an ally of Germany.

Great Britain was a much weaker country after the war, and was unable to suppress the movements for independence in many of its colonies around the world. Most of these colonies soon

**Samuel Beckett
(1906–1989)**
Waiting For Godot

**William Golding
(1911–1993)**
Lord of the Flies

**Dylan Thomas
(1914–1953)**
Poems

**Anthony Burgess
(1917–1993)**
A Clockwork Orange

**Doris Lessing
(1919–)**
The Golden Notebook

JAMES JOYCE (1882–1941)

Irish with a Catholic background (he was educated in Jesuit Schools), Joyce is another key writer in the Modernist period (the first half of the twentieth century). He experimented with language and the novel form, and along with Virginia Woolf, was one of the champions of stream-of-consciousness writing. This style of writing is narrative that attempts to reflect the way we think rather than the way traditional narrative forms (once upon a time...then this happened...then that...The End) tell us we think. His work is full of puns, symbols, double meanings, and unpunctuated bodies of text. In other words, it's really hard to read. In *Ulysses*, his most famous novel, Joyce uses the framework of Homer's *Odyssey* to describe a single day in the lives of three characters. If you want a less intimidating start, try *Dubliners*, a collection of perfectly crafted (so perfectly crafted you might find them lifeless) short stories set in his hometown. If you love Joyce, you'll probably hate Lawrence, and vice versa.

became independent countries. Many of the writers of these countries, such as **V. S. Naipaul** from Trinidad, Nigeria's **Chinua Achebe**, and India's **Salman Rushdie**, continue to write in English. Many of the writers in former British colonies use their stories and poems to explore racism, nationalism, and their people's experience of living under British colonial rule.

GEORGE ORWELL (1903–1950)

Big Brother. Newspeak. Thoughtcrime. You've probably heard these terms before—they come from the novel, *1984*, the masterpiece of Eric Blair, better known to you as George Orwell. *1984* portrays a futuristic world in which a totalitarian government controls every aspect of life, including thought. This novel was so influential that the word *Orwellian* arose to refer to situations, behavior, or policies that are oppressive and beyond individual control.

Born in Bengal, Orwell grew up a lonely kid in England. He served as a police officer with the Indian Imperial Police in Burma, lived in severe poverty in Paris and London, fought as a volunteer against the fascist forces in the Spanish Civil War, and wrote constantly all the while. At the age of 47, he died of—you guessed it—tuberculosis.

Orwell's great gift was the expression of fiercely held beliefs and ideas in some of the most lucid and efficient English you're likely to come across. His beliefs had been solidified by his experience fighting in Spain. From that point on, he wrote, "I knew where I stood. Every line of serious work that I have written since 1936 has been written, directly or indirectly, *against* totalitarianism and *for* democratic socialism." Both of his great political satires, *Animal Farm* and *1984*, dwell on human beings' intrinsic capacity for cruelty. The view in *1984* is bleak, the message terrifying: Too many of the social models we've come up with encourage our inner desire for power, toward which we move at the expense of our humanity.

6

A Selective Timeline of American Literature

Timelines serve one purpose: They show information *at a glance.* If you can never remember whether Wordsworth was a Romantic, or Pope a satirist—if you don't know your Rationalism from your Modernism, your Regency from your Renaissance—a timeline is what you need. In the following pages you'll find the basics: writers, what they wrote, and what was going on (politically, economically, etc.), while they were writing. There are no lengthy expositions of particular works, nor are there any tips on how to read the authors in the timeline. Instead, there's a simple chronology of who was doing what and when they were doing it.

When using this chapter, there are two things to keep in mind. First, this is a *selective* timeline. It is by no means exhaustive as a list of writers or their works. It focuses on writers and works you're likely to encounter (or at least hear of) in high school or college. So don't go away with the impression that Melville, for example, *only* wrote *Moby Dick*, or that Joseph Heller *only* wrote *Catch-22*, or that there were no other writers between Stephen Crane and Theodore Dreiser who were of any significance or merit. Remember: It's a rough guide.

Second, it's important to realize that "historical periods" don't generally begin and end abruptly. In this timeline, for example, you'll see Civil War and Realism (1860–1900) followed by Modernism (1900–1950). Don't get hung up on the dividing lines between the periods. They are approximate.

THE PURITANS, RATIONALISTS, AND THE REVOLUTION (1600–1800)

One of the first major American literary works was *The Scarlet Letter*, written by **Nathaniel Hawthorne**. Although Hawthorne didn't write his novel until the mid-nineteenth century, it reflects an earlier time in the United States, the era of the Puritans, some of the first European settlers of the new country. The Puritans had left England for America to escape persecution and to set up their ideal society. The word *puritan* comes from the efforts of this group of people,

NATHANIEL HAWTHORNE (1804–1864)

Nathaniel Hawthorne was not the kind of guy you'd want to invite to a party. When he graduated from Bowdoin College in Maine, he wrote to his sister Elizabeth that, "I shall never make a distinguished figure in the world, and all I hope or wish is to plod along with the multitude." While Hawthorne's gloomy prediction about his future would be proved wrong, he was moody through much of his life and liked to spend a lot of his time alone. He had grown up in Salem, Massachusetts, as the child of a widowed mother with little money. After college, where he spent most of his time playing cards and drinking, he moved back to his childhood house and holed up in an upstairs room, which he called the "dismal chamber." For the next 12 years, he spent most of his time in that room working on his fiction. In 1837, he published a collection of stories, but it didn't make him enough money to live on. For a short time, Hawthorne tried living on a communal farm that was part of the Transcendentalists' experiment in utopian living, but he gave up on it. In 1842, he married Sophia Peabody, whom he appeared to love well and who loved him. They spent most of their lives in Concord, Massachusetts, where he wrote *The Scarlet Letter*—which he described as a "hell-fired story, into which I found it almost impossible to throw any cheering light."

who were Protestants, to "purify" the Church of England. They didn't feel that the changes brought about by the Reformation (see The Renaissance, pg. 113) were enough. The Puritans believed that religious observance should be simpler, that each person had a private, individual relationship with God that didn't depend on the rituals or words of a priest or minister. They wanted to live as closely to the Bible as possible, believing strongly that because Adam and Eve had sinned, human beings should spend their lives working to live sin-free in the hope of salvation. They judged people who they called "sinners" very harshly, such as the protagonist in *The Scarlet Letter*, Hester Prynne, who was punished for adultery. A group of women in Salem, Massachusetts, were even accused of being witches by zealous Puritan leaders, who found the behavior or attitudes of the women unacceptable or strange. They were hanged in 1691 and 1692. Their story was told by a contemporary author, **Arthur Miller**, in his play, *The Crucible*.

The writing of the era itself was essentially nonfictional, with many of the Puritans maintaining diaries and histories to monitor their feelings and look for signs of God among the events in their lives and their communities. Other writings of the time were the accounts of colonists who said that they had been captured by Native Americans. These "captivity" stories, which were widely read in England as well as in the colonies, were often exaggerated, and by the early nineteenth century, most of the stories were made up. Most of these stories described European settlers being tortured by Native Americans, which encouraged hostility toward Native Americans and led to stereotypes of them as "savages."

The American independence movement, which culminated in the Revolutionary War (1775–1783), resulted in a variety of political pamphlets and essays. Many of these writers, such as **Benjamin Franklin** and **Thomas Jefferson**, were not Puritans but were part of a movement called *Rationalism*. Similar to the trend in Europe during the Enlightenment, Rationalists had complete faith in the human intellect; they valued reason above all else, and believed that people were essentially good and capable of creating an ideal society.

AMERICAN ROMANTICISM AND THE RENAISSANCE (1800–1860)

American **Romantic writers**, like their European counterparts, came to rebel against the ideas of the **Rationalists**. They valued emotion, imagination, and intuition above reason and found much inspiration in nature. Just as European Romantics were responding to the grim reality of the Industrial Revolution, American Romantics reacted to the reality of nation-building in the Industrial Age, such as the loss of natural beauty as a result of the quick rise of new American cities. **Romantic poets** like **Henry Wadsworth Longfellow**, **Oliver Wendell Holmes**, and **John**

Washington Irving (1783–1859)
The Sketch Book, containing "The Legend of Sleepy Hollow"

EDGAR ALLAN POE (1809–1849)

Although Edgar Allan Poe's work was the precursor to the modern detective story—inspiring Sherlock Holmes' creator, Arthur Conan Doyle—this early master of suspenseful storytelling was unable to master his own life. He had a rough start: He was orphaned at age 3, and had a difficult relationship with his foster father. He joined and then had himself dismissed from the U.S. Military Academy at West Point. He moved in with an aunt in Baltimore in 1835 and then married her 13-year-old daughter, Virginia (Poe was 26). He tried to support his family by working as a magazine editor, but they were often poor and Poe was an alcoholic. After Virginia died of tuberculosis in 1847, Poe discovered that he had a terminal brain lesion. In an ending that would have fit perfectly in one of his stories about a hero haunted by his own mind, in 1849, Poe, who had gone missing for a week, was discovered in a Baltimore bar; his clothes were ripped and wet and he was incoherent from drinking. Before he died four days later, he prayed: "Lord help my poor soul."

HENRY DAVID THOREAU (1817–1862)

 From his cabin in the woods surrounding Walden Pond in Massachusetts, Henry David Thoreau thought about the life he had left behind. "The mass of men," he wrote, "lead lives of quiet desperation." Thoreau had come to the woods as an experiment, to see what it felt like to live in a solitary way close to nature. He lived and wrote in a tiny cabin for most of 2 years, contemplating Transcendentalism (see American Romanticism and the Renaissance [1800–1860]). Although *Walden*, his memoir of his experience, became an important American literary work, his friends felt that he had wasted his time. But his retreat into the woods had probably been good news for his acquaintance Nathaniel Hawthorne, who once wrote that Thoreau was "tedious, tiresome, and intolerable." He added, however, that Thoreau "has great qualities of intellect and character." This character was revealed when he went to jail as the result of refusing to pay taxes in protest against the Mexican War, as well as helping African Americans escape slavery by moving them along the Underground Railroad to Canada. His essay, *Resistance to Civil Government*, helped inspire India's Mohandas Gandhi and Martin Luther King, Jr.

Greenleaf Whittier were very popular and came to be known as the *Fireside Poets*, because their work was often read by families sitting together in front of their fireplace (a pre-TV family activity). But this group of writers stayed within the traditional, European mode of poetry writing, hoping to prove to readers and critics in Great Britain that American writers were just as good as English writers. The first American novelists, however, such as **James Fenimore Cooper**, celebrated American explorers' wisdom, resourcefulness, and respect for the North American wilderness, creating new, distinctly American heroes in their writing.

It was not until the mid-1800s that the American literary renaissance really took off. This was the time that American literature began to take shape, with the publishing of books by **Nathaniel Hawthorne, Herman Melville, Edgar Allan Poe, Ralph Waldo Emerson**, and **Henry David Thoreau**, and the poets **Emily Dickinson** and **Walt Whitman**. Although many of these authors published during the same period—between

James Fenimore Cooper (1789–1851)
The Deerslayer
The Last of The Mohicans

Ralph Waldo Emerson (1803–1882)
Essays, *containing "Self-Reliance"*
Nature
Poems

Nathaniel Hawthorne (1804–1864)
The Scarlet Letter

Henry Wadsworth Longfellow (1807–1882)
Poems
Hiawatha

WALT WHITMAN (1819–1892)

Walt Whitman, who was America's first literary star and the originator of free verse, went to school until the ripe old age of 11. While growing up in West Hills, Long Island (now the town of Huntington), he worked at odd office jobs, using his time off to stroll along Long Island's beaches. On his own he read the Bible, Shakespeare, and the Greek classics. He later worked as a journalist and then took a break from that and deepened his knowledge of the American wilderness while traveling down to New Orleans and back up to Michigan. He eventually moved to Brooklyn, New York, and worked as an editor, carpenter, and building contractor. On the side, he kept a journal and worked on the passionate, free verse, free-thinking poems that would rock the world of poetry. But in 1855, when he was ready to share his work with the world, no one was very interested. To many critics, it didn't even seem like poetry. He published his collection, the now famous *Leaves of Grass*, at his own expense. He tried to call attention to the book by sending it to famous writers, such as Ralph Waldo Emerson. It was a good move. Emerson wrote back that he found it "the most extraordinary piece of wit and wisdom that America has yet contributed. . . . I greet you at the beginning of a great career." Although he was an ardent self-promoter, Whitman was an energetic, well-liked, life-loving man who, as one contemporary described him, "always had the look of a man who had just taken a bath."

Edgar Allan Poe (1809–1849)
The Raven and Other Poems
"The Fall of the House of Usher"
"The Tell Tale Heart"
"The Cask of Amontillado"

Henry David Thoreau (1817–1862)
Walden

Herman Melville (1819–1891)
Moby Dick

Emily Dickinson (1830–1886)
Poems

1840 and 1860—their work reflects very different thinking about religion, human nature, and the future. This was a time when many Americans, who lived primarily in New England, were attending meetings in barns, schools, and churches to talk about how best to organize American society. There were movements for better public education, an end to slavery, and women's rights. One of the top speakers on the lecture circuit at the time was writer Ralph Waldo Emerson, who, along with Henry David Thoreau, was part of a movement called *Transcendentalism*. They believed that to live a more satisfying life, you had to go beyond, or transcend, everyday reality, by immersing yourself in the mystery of nature. They were optimistic, putting much faith in the power of the individual. Emerson and others believed that people could be happy and good if they felt a personal connection to nature, which, in their view, meant that they had found a personal connection to God. By contrast, writers like Herman Melville, Edgar Allan Poe, and

EMILY DICKINSON (1830–1886)

 In 1861, after years of living and writing in virtual seclusion, Emily Dickinson wrote, "I'm Nobody! Who are you? / Are you—Nobody—too?" Ego was not, to say the least, one of Dickinson's problems. She never knew how important her poetry would become for readers around the world. Few poems were published during her lifetime. She wrote mainly for family and close friends, and rarely left her family home in Amherst, Massachusetts, after 1862. The reasons why Dickinson began to wear only white and became a recluse when she was still young remain a mystery. One of the theories was that she never recovered from falling in love with a married pastor who later moved far away from her. But she remained an enigma in many ways; although she told her family to destroy her poems after her death, she hid small bundles of poems around her house. The full genius of her work was finally discovered after her death. Although she never went much beyond her home, she saw the whole universe in the grass, clouds, sun, insects, and animals outside her window.

Nathaniel Hawthorne had less faith in humanity. Many of their stories, using fantasy and symbolism, focus on human suffering and reflect their interest in what drives people to do evil things.

Louisa May Alcott (1832–1888)
Little Women

THE CIVIL WAR AND REALISM (1850–1900)

In the early 1850s, a decade before the Civil War, writings about slavery began to be published. In 1850 the Fugitive Slave Act was passed, which imposed punishment on anyone who helped a person trying to escape enslavement in the southern states. The next year, **Harriet Beecher Stowe** wrote a novel about slavery called *Uncle Tom's Cabin*, which prompted nationwide debate and, say some historians, helped trigger the war. Before Stowe's novel, however, the reality of slavery was powerfully documented in *The Narrative of the Life of Frederick Douglass, An American Slave*, which **Frederick Douglass** published in 1845. That was followed in 1850 by the life story of **Sojourner Truth**, a woman who had once been a slave and then worked hard to abolish slavery and improve women's rights.

Harriet Beecher Stowe (1811–1896)
Uncle Tom's Cabin

Walt Whitman (1819–1892)
Leaves of Grass
Poems

Mark Twain (1835–1910)
The Adventures of Huckleberry Finn

**Frederick Douglass
(1817–1895)**
*The Narrative of the Life
of Frederick Douglass, an
American Slave*

**Henry James
(1843–1916)**
The Portrait of a Lady

**Kate Chopin
(1851–1904)**
The Awakening

**Edith Wharton
(1862–1937)**
*Ethan Frome
The Age of Innocence*

**Stephen Crane
(1871–1900)**
The Red Badge of Courage

On April 12, 1861, troops from a coalition of Southern states fired on Fort Sumter, beginning their drive to secede from the United States. The four-year war inspired some writers, like poet **Walt Whitman**, to celebrate the resilience and bravery of U.S. soldiers just as his prewar poetry had reflected his belief in a bold American spirit. But while Whitman maintained faith in the America after the war, **Herman Melville** was one of the writers who focused on human beings' self-destructive capabilities and became more pessimistic about the future.

The most important writer about the Civil War, however, was **Stephen Crane**, who published *The Red Badge of Courage* in 1895. His novel represented an important new trend in writing called *Realism*, which is reflected in much of the fiction we read today. Crane and others tried to describe real life as accurately as possible. Unlike the Romantics, they resisted bringing their personal ideology into their writing, trying instead to more neutrally observe and explore the lives of ordinary people. These writers were interested in the new fields of psychology and biology. Both Stephen Crane and **Henry James** were masters of what is called the *psychological novel*. They were fascinated with what motivates people to behave they way they do, and they liked to describe what was really going on in people's minds as they did everyday things. Other writers, such as **Mark Twain**, were regionalists, focusing on the reality of life in certain parts of the country. His famous novel, *Huckleberry Finn*, offered a complex portrait of relationships between the races in the South.

F. SCOTT FITZGERALD (1896–1940)

F. Scott Fitzgerald lived the life he wrote about—fun, luxurious, and over the top. He helped coin the phrase the "Jazz Age," working hard with his wife Zelda to turn the 1920s into the Roaring '20s. Fitzgerald had grown up in a wealthy family in St. Paul, Minnesota, and was a failure in school and sports. He began writing stories and plays when he was still a teenager and kept at it when he went to Princeton. Looking for adventure, he left college in 1917 when World War I broke out, but he was never sent overseas. He was stationed instead at Camp Sheridan in Alabama and fell in love with Zelda Sayre, a woman who was as wild at heart as he was. They later moved to New York, where they went to a lot of parties and he wrote. And wrote. Finally he told his editor that he planned to write "something new—something extraordinary and beautiful and simple and intricately patterned." It was *The Great Gatsby*, which was published in 1925. But his insight into the often hollow, self-destructive lives of the rich and glamorous set didn't do much for his own life. Zelda had a mental breakdown in 1930 and was in and out of asylums for the rest of her life. Fitzgerald went into debt, struggled with alcoholism and depression, and died of heart failure in 1940 as he was trying to finish *The Last Tycoon*.

MODERNISM (1900–1950)

After World War I (1914–1918) and the Great Depression, which began in 1929, Americans' core beliefs about themselves and the world began to change. The "American dream"—the idea that individuals can take advantage of America's abundant resources and opportunities and build a good life if they only work hard enough—didn't seem so true anymore. During the the early thirties, at least one-fourth of all workers were unemployed. People stood in long lines waiting for bread and whole families slept in tents, shacks, or on the streets. More people were cynical about government statements and began to question traditional ways of thinking about politics and culture. The development of Marxism and the spread of Sigmund Freud's ideas (see The Twen-

Theodore Dreiser (1871–1945)
An American Tragedy

Willa Cather (1873–1947)
O Pioneers!
My Antonia

Robert Frost (1874–1963)
Poems, including
"The Road Not Taken"

William Carlos Williams (1883–1963)
Poems

Sinclair Lewis (1885–1951)
Main Street
Babbitt

Ezra Pound (1885–1972)
Cantos

Eugene O'Neill (1888-1953)
Long Day's Journey into Night

T. S. Eliot (1888–1965)
Poems
The Waste Land

Katherine Ann Porter (1890–1980)
Pale Horse, Pale Rider
Ship of Fools

tieth Century, pg. 121) further challenged conventional ideas about politics, economics, and human nature. The stream-of-consciousness style of writers like **William Faulkner** and **Katherine Anne Porter**, following the lead of Ireland's **James Joyce**, was influenced by Freud and the developing field of psychology.

Other writers were focusing on the reality of American life. **Sinclair Lewis**, in his satiric 1920 novel, *Main Street*, challenged the myth of the idyllic small American town. The work of **Ernest Hemingway** had a major influence on American literature because of his plain, no-nonsense style of writing and his disillusionment with American ideals. **F. Scott Fitzgerald**, a contemporary of Hemingway, explored the consequences of trying to live the American dream, questioning society's definition of success and progress in his novel, *The Great Gatsby*.

At the same time there was also a spirit of change and growth, particularly during the Roaring '20s, that was reflected in the literature of the time. The poetry of **T. S. Eliot, Ezra Pound, e. e. cummings**, and **Marianne Moore** broke from tra-

ZORA NEALE HURSTON (C. 1891–1960)

When Zora Neale Hurston arrived in New York City in 1925 to go to Barnard College, she had a dollar and a half to her name. Hurston's desire to live close to the edge was clear when she was a girl growing up in the all-black town of Eatonville, Florida. "It grew upon me that I ought to walk out to the horizon," she wrote in her autobiography, "and see what the end of the world was like." After her mother died when Hurston was 9 years old, Hurston lived with various relatives and had to begin to support herself in the beginning of her teens. She arrived in New York after attending Washington, D.C.'s Howard University, where she had begun writing fiction. By the time she hit New York, Hurston was ready for it. The Harlem Renaissance (see Modernism) was in full swing and she jumped into the middle of it: dancing, giving parties, dressing up in dramatic hats and turbans, and, of course, writing. She wrote plays and stories and later traveled through the South to collect and preserve African American folk tales. In 1937 she published her most important work, *Their Eyes Were Watching God*, about a young African American woman who rejects the traditional expectation that she get married and settle down in order to live as full a life as possible.

JOHN STEINBECK (1902–1968)

Many writers of the 1930s tried to write about the Great Depression, but John Steinbeck was one of the few who wrote memorably. Whereas many prominent writers of the time were from the East Coast, Steinbeck's perspective was unique; he grew up in California's Salinas Valley, the son of a schoolteacher and a county treasurer. In addition to attending Stanford for a short time, Steinbeck worked as a fruit picker, surveyor, laboratory assistant, and journalist, among many other jobs. For a few years he went to work with a group of Oklahoma farmers, an experience that would inspire his greatest work. He grew angry at a system that benefited big company farms at the expense of small, independent farmers, who often ended up losing their land and having to travel to find work as hired help. The struggles of migrant workers became the subject of his Pulitzer Prize–winning novel, *The Grapes of Wrath*, which was published in 1939. He won the Nobel Prize in literature in 1962.

dition and embodied a "modern" style that was more impersonal and began to use symbolism to a greater degree. This trend in literature was influenced by European modernist artists such as Pablo Picasso and Henri Matisse, whose work was a radical departure from what had come before.

The 1920s was also the time during which many African Americans migrated to northern cities, which was one of the factors that led to what has been called the *Harlem Renaissance*. Harlem was, and still is, a predominately African American community in the New York City borough of Manhattan. After the great northern migration, many writers, artists, and musicians came together in Harlem and often influenced each other's work. These artists focused on the reality of black life and history, racism, and American identity, among many other themes. Among the most prominent writers of the time were the lyric poets **Langston Hughes, James Weldon Johnson**, and **Countee Cullen**, and later novelists **Zora Neale Hurston** and **Richard Wright**.

The year 1920 was also the year that women finally won the right to vote under the Nine-

Ernest Hemingway (1899–1961)
A Farewell to Arms
The Old Man and the Sea

Thomas Wolfe (1900–1938)
Look Homeward Angel
Of Time and River
The Web and the Rock

Langston Hughes (1902–1967)
Poems

John Steinbeck (1902–1968)
Of Mice and Men
The Grapes of Wrath

Robert Penn Warren (1905–1989)
All the King's Men

W. H. Auden (1907–1973)
Poems

teenth Amendment to the U.S. Constitution. This era of new opportunities for women was reflected in the poetry of writers like **Edna St. Vincent Millay**, who believed that women should have the same personal freedom as men. In 1923, she became the first woman to win the Pulitzer Prize in poetry.

CONTEMPORARY LITERATURE AND POSTMODERNISM (1950 TO THE PRESENT)

With the dropping of an atomic bomb on the Japanese city of Hiroshima on August 6, 1945, World War II came to an end. But the wartime sense of national unity, patriotism, and faith in government continued through the 1950s. Although the war with Germany was over, this was the beginning of the Cold War with the Soviet Union, and the idea of nuclear war became possible. The tendency of most Americans to conform to traditional ways of thinking led some poets in the 1950s and 1960s to develop new, nonconformist ways of writing. **Robert Lowell,**

SYLVIA PLATH (1932–1963)

Although Sylvia Plath died when she was only 31, the poetry she left behind was "triumphant," in the words of fellow poet Robert Lowell. He also described her work as "appalling"—not because it was bad, but because it revealed the depth of her emotional pain. Plath had her first poem published in a Boston newspaper when she was 8 years old. It was close to the time that her father died from diabetes, a tragedy that, by some accounts, Plath viewed as the source of her life-long struggle with depression. But she was a dedicated and ambitious writer—she received 45 rejection letters from *Seventeen* magazine before they accepted one of her short stories. She later received a scholarship to Smith College and won a fiction prize from *Mademoiselle* magazine. Not long after, she attempted suicide for the first time. She received electroshock as treatment; drug therapy for manic depression had not yet been developed. She went on to Cambridge University in England and married a British poet, Ted Hughes, in 1956; they had two children and later separated. In 1963, she published *The Bell Jar*, an autobiographical novel about her battle against depression. That same year, in an unheated London apartment during an extremely cold winter, Plath killed herself.

Anne Sexton, Sylvia Plath, and **John Berryman** were among those who rejected T. S. Eliot's impersonal, "objective," modernist style and wrote boldly honest poems that revealed much more about their lives and feelings. As a result, they became part of what was called the *Confessional School*.

In 1956, poet **Allen Ginsberg** appeared on the scene. He and others working in a similar vein, who came to be called the *Beat Poets*, used their writing to more directly reflect the rebellious, imaginative spirit of the 1960s. The Vietnam War was bitterly opposed by many people and led to the growing rejection of conventional attitudes toward war, government, and capitalism. **Joseph Heller's** 1961 novel, *Catch-22*, used World War II to examine the insanity of war itself. More people were also questioning traditional views of marriage, sex, and women's role in society, and this intensified during the activism of the women's movement in the 1970s.

The 1980s have recently been dubbed the "me generation" to reflect the movement away from the social and political activism of the 1960s and 1970s and the growing focus on individual wealth. The 1980s and 1990s have also been the decades in which advances in technology have touched everyone's lives, from the development of personal computers to the Internet. The new technologies of the information age have made the global economy possible while leading to the elimination of many jobs, a widening gap between rich and poor, and anxiety about the future. Against this backdrop, today's writers are trying more to raise questions than to answer them. Their work reflects a cultural trend called *postmodernism*, which values new, experimental forms of writing and the blending of fiction with nonfiction; rejects objective notions of "truth"; and embraces the stories of people from varying backgrounds and cultures, whose experiences offer unique perspectives on life.

**J. D. Salinger
(1919–)**
*The Catcher in the Rye
Nine Stories
Franny and Zooey*

**Joseph Heller
(1923–)**
Catch-22

**James Baldwin
(1924–1987)**
*Go Tell It On the
Mountain
Another Country
Just Above My Head*

**Allen Ginsberg
(1926–1997)**
Howl and Other Poems

**Ann Sexton
(1928–1974)**
Poems

**E. L. Doctorow
(1931–)**
*The Book of Daniel
Ragtime*

**Toni Morrison
[Chloe Anthony
Wofford]
(1931–)**
*Song of Solomon
Beloved
Jazz*

**Sylvia Plath
(1932–1963)**
*Collected Poems
The Bell Jar*

CHAPTER 7

A Glossary of Literary Terms

allegory—A story in which characters represent abstract qualities or ideas. For example, in *Superman* comics, Superman represents good, and all the bad guys he fights represent evil.

alliteration—The repetition of first consonants in a group of words, as in "*B*ah, *b*ah, *b*lack sheep."

allusion—A reference to something or someone, often literary. When you say "You watch what you say or I'll bite your ear off," you are making an *allusion* to the infamous Tyson-Holyfield fight, in which Tyson bit off part of Holyfield's ear. The verb form of allusion is to **allude**.

assonance—The repetition of vowel sounds, as in "p*a*le-f*a*ce J*a*ke."

atmosphere—The overall feeling of a work, related to tone and mood.

blank verse—Unrhymed lines of poetry (usually in **iambic pentameter**—10-syllable lines in which every other syllable is stressed). Much of the poetry written today is in blank verse.

characterization—The means by which an author establishes character. An author can directly describe a character's personality and appearance or can show it through dialogue and actions.

climax—The point at which the action in a story or play reaches its emotional peak.

conflict—The forces that give rise to a plot. Traditionally, every plot is built from the most basic elements of a conflict and an eventual resolution. The conflict can be internal (within one character) or external (among characters or between characters and nature, for example).

contrast—To say how two things are different. To **compare and contrast** is to say how two things are alike and how they are different.

couplets—A pair of rhyming lines in a poem, often set off from the rest of the poem. Shakespeare's sonnets all end in *couplets*.

denouement—Literally "untying a knot," this term refers to the resolution of the conflict in a plot after the climax. It also refers to the action in a story or play after the principal drama is resolved.

dramatic monologue—A poem with a fictional narrator, addressed to someone whose identity the audience knows, but who doesn't say anything. A lot of love songs could be considered dramatic monologues: We need only look as far as that maestro of the overblown love ballad, Barry Manilow ("Well you came and you gave without taking, but I sent you away, oh Mandy").

elegy—A poem mourning the dead.

end rhyme—Just what it sounds like: rhyming words that are at the ends of their respective lines. Basically, what you probably think of as normal rhyme.

epic—A long poem narrating the adventures of a heroic figure, for example *The Iliad* and *The Odyssey* by Homer.

fable—A story that illustrates a moral, often using animals as the characters.

figurative language—Language that is not **literal**, that is, that does not mean exactly what it says. For example, when you offer someone a ride by saying "Hop in," you don't literally mean that you'd like them to jump into your car on one foot, so you're using *figurative language*. **Metaphors** and **similes** are both types of *figurative language*.

first person—The point of view of a piece of writing in which the narrator refers to himself as "I." A first-person narrative might begin with something like, "When I woke up that morning." A piece written in the **second person** refers to the main character as "you " and might begin with a line like "When you woke up this morning." (The second person is pretty rare, but if you've ever read *Bright Lights, Big City* by Jay McInerney, you know all about it.) A piece written in the **third person** refers to all of the characters as "he" or "she."

foreshadowing—A technique in which an author gives clues about something that will happen later in the plot.

free verse—Poetry with no set meter (rhythm) or rhyme scheme.

genre—A kind or style, usually of art or literature. Examples of genres of literature are the novel, play, satire, lyric poem, and comedy of errors.

hyperbole—Great exaggeration, as in, "I'm so hungry I could eat a horse" or "He's as big as a house."

imagery—The use of description that helps the reader imagine how something sounds, feels, smells, tastes, or (most often) looks. An **image** is the thing being described.

internal rhyme—A rhyme that occurs within one line, as in "I have a new game said the Cat in the Hat" (Dr. Seuss, *The Cat in the Hat*).

irony—Language that conveys a certain idea by saying just the opposite. If, for example, a king responded to the news that his palace was under siege by saying "How delightful that they've all dropped in for a visit," we could assume that he was being ironic.

literal—Meaning exactly what it says. If someone says "I'm going to leave quickly," she is being literal; if she says "I'm going to leave so fast it will make your head spin," she is not being literal (instead, she is using **figurative language**).

lyric—A type of poetry that expresses the poet's emotions. It often tells some sort of brief story, engaging the reader in the experience.

metaphor—A comparison that doesn't use "like" or "as"—for example, "I am a rock, I am an island."

meter—The pattern of stressed and unstressed syllables in the lines of a poem.

monologue—A long speech by one character in a play or story.

mood—The emotional atmosphere of a given piece of writing.

motif—A theme or pattern that recurs in a work.

myth—A legend, usually partly made up of historical events, that embodies the beliefs of a people and offers some explanation for natural and social phenomena.

onomatopoeia—The use of words that sound like what they mean, like "snap," "crackle," and "pop."

oxymoron—A phrase made up of two seemingly opposite words: "grand depression," or "burning ice."

paradox—A seeming contradiction, like the opening lines of Charles Dickens' *A Tale of Two Cities*: "It was the best of times, it was the worst of times."

parody—A humorous, exaggerated imitation of another work.

personification—Talking about a nonhuman thing as if it were human, as in, "The morning light mocked our poor hero."

plot—The story line, or what happens in the story. For example, you could summarize the plot of J. D. Salinger's *The Catcher in the Rye* as "Holden gets expelled from school and wanders around in New York."

prose—Written expression that is organized into sentences and paragraphs. What we consider normal writing—no rhyme and no specific meter.

protagonist—The main character of a novel, play, or story.

pun—The use of a word in a way that plays on its different meanings, like "What do you call a sheep dipped in chocolate? A candy bah!" Get it? Candy bah? Candy bar? That's a pun. Or, as in this case, plays on the words sounding like another word.

quatrain—A four-line stanza.

rhetorical question—A question that's not meant to be answered, such as "Who does he think he is?"

satire—A work that makes fun of something or someone. Most *Saturday Night Live* skits could be described as **satiric**, for example, because they make fun of movies, current events, and public figures.

sensory imagery—Imagery that has to do with something you could see, hear, taste, smell, or feel, like "the velvety sand" or "the salty air."

simile—A comparison that uses "like" or "as," as in "She is like the wind."

soliloquy—A monologue in which a character expresses his or her thoughts to the audience and does not intend the other characters to hear them.

sonnet—A fourteen-line poem written in **iambic pentameter** (ten-syllable lines in which every other syllable is stressed). Different kinds of sonnets have different rhyme schemes.

stanza—A section of poetry, separated from the sections that come before and after it. A verse paragraph.

subplot—A secondary plot in a story.

symbolism—The use of one thing to represent another. For example, hearts are often used to symbolize love, skulls to symbolize death.

theme—The central idea of a work. For example, one of the major themes of *The Wizard of Oz* is that there's no place like home.

tone—The author's attitude toward his or her subject.

voice—The narrator's particular way of speaking. A narrator's voice can be formal, colloquial, humorous, etc.

Practice Exams
and Explanations

PRACTICE EXAM ONE

PART 1

READING COMPREHENSION

The following passage is adapted from a 1942 speech by the British novelist and essayist Virginia Woolf, entitled "Professions for Women."

When your secretary invited me to come here, she told me that your group is concerned with the employment of women, and she suggested that I might tell you something about my own professional experiences. Many famous women, and many more unknown and forgotten, have been before me, making the path smooth, and regulating my steps. Thus, when I came to write, there were very few material obstacles in my way. Writing was a reputable and harmless occupation. The family peace was not broken by the scratching of a pen. No demand was made upon the family purse. For ten and sixpence one can buy paper enough to write all the plays of Shakespeare. The cheapness of writing paper is, of course, the reason why women have succeeded as writers before they have succeeded in other professions.

But to tell you my story—it is a simple one. You have only got to imagine a girl in a bedroom with a pen in her hand. She had only to move that pen from left to right—from ten o'clock to one. Then it occurred to her to do what is simple and cheap enough after all—to slip a few pages of those into an envelope, fix a penny stamp in the corner, and drop the envelope into the box at the corner. It was thus that I became a journalist; and my effort was rewarded on the first day of the following month—by a letter from an editor containing a check. But to show you how little I deserve to be called a professional woman, how little I know the struggles and difficulties of such lives, I have to admit that instead of spending that sum on bread and butter, rent, or butcher's bills, I went out and bought a cat—a beautiful Persian cat, which very soon involved me in bitter disputes with my neighbors.

What could be easier than to write articles and buy Persian cats with the profits? But wait a moment. Articles have to be about something. Mine, I seem to remember, was about a novel by a famous man. And while I was writing this review, I discovered that if I were going to review books I should need to do battle with a certain phantom. The phantom was a woman, and when I came to know her better I came to call her after a heroine of a famous poem, "The Angel in the House." It was she who used to come between me and my paper when I was writing reviews. It was she who bothered me and wasted my time and so tormented me that at last I killed her. You who come of a younger and happier generation may not have heard of her—you may not know what I mean by "The Angel in the House." I will describe her as shortly as I can. She was intensely sympathetic, immensely charming, and utterly unselfish. She sacrificed herself daily. If there was chicken, she took the leg. If there was a draft, she sat in it—in short she was so constituted that she never had a mind or wish of her own, but preferred to sympathize always with the minds and wishes of others. Above all—she was pure. Her purity was supposed to be her chief beauty—her blushes, her great grace. In those days—the last of Queen Victoria—every house had its Angel. And when I came to write I encountered her with the very first words. The shadows of her wings fell on my page; I heard the rustling of her skirts in the room. As soon as I took my pen in hand to review that novel by a famous man, she slipped behind me and whispered: "My dear, you are a young woman. You are writing about a book that has been written by a man. Be sympathetic; be tender; flatter; deceive; use all the arts and wiles of our sex. Never let anybody guess that you have a mind of your own. Above all, be pure." And she made as if to guide my pen.

I now record the one act for which I take some credit to myself, though the credit rightly belongs to some excellent ancestors of mine who left me a certain sum of money—so that it was not necessary for me to depend solely on charm for my living. I turned upon her and caught her by the throat. I did my best to kill her. My excuse, if I were to be had up in a court of law, would be that I acted in self-defense. Had I not killed her she would have killed me. She would have plucked the heart out of my writing. I found directly I put pen to paper, you cannot review even a novel without having a mind of your own, without expressing what you think to be the truth about human relations, or morality. All these questions, according to "The Angel in the House," cannot be dealt with freely and openly by a woman; they must tell lies if they are to proceed. Thus, whenever I felt the shadow of her wing or the radiance of her halo on my page, I took up the inkpot and flung it at her. She died hard. Her fictitious nature was of great assistance to her. It is far harder to kill a phantom than a reality. She was always creeping back when I thought I had dispatched her. But it was a real experience, an experience that was bound to befall all women writers at the time. Killing "The Angel in the House" was part of the occupation of a woman writer.

1 In her opening lines, Woolf attributes her smooth entrance into her profession to
   1 an encouraging editor
   2 a lack of competition
   3 guidance from friends
   4 women writers of the past

2 According to Woolf, writing was considered a suitable occupation for women because it
   1 generated additional income for the family
   2 brought fame to the family
   3 caused little strain on the family
   4 provided entertainment for the family

3 Who does Woolf imply is the girl in the bedroom?
   1 a family member   3 Woolf herself
   2 a female friend   4 an imaginary writer

4 Woolf says she became a journalist when
   1 an editor offered her a job
   2 she sent an article to an editor
   3 she applied for an advertised position
   4 a friend submitted her writing to a publisher

5 As recalled by Woolf, what form did her early writings take?
   1 book reviews   3 novels
   2 poems   4 mystery stories

6 Woolf portrays "The Angel in the House" as being
   1 honest   3 inquisitive
   2 self-reliant   4 self-sacrificing

7 In describing the angel as "pure," Woolf most likely means the angel is
   1 young   3 virtuous
   2 frivolous   4 plain

8 In "killing" the angel, Woolf was trying to preserve her own
   1 status   3 sanity
   2 integrity   4 history

9 In spite of the name Angel in the House, Woolf's angel is really
   1 an obstacle   3 a flirt
   2 a traitor   4 a coward

10 The Angel in the House most nearly represents the
  1 poetic muse
  2 spirit of other women writers
  3 author's approaching death
  4 ideal woman of the time

VOCABULARY

Directions (11–30): Choose the number of the word or phrase that most nearly expresses the meaning of the word printed in heavy black type. [10]

11 **endorsement**
  1 obedience
  2 approval
  3 resignation
  4 compromise

12 **corrosive**
  1 slowly destructive
  2 highly prejudiced
  3 generally distrustful
  4 rather ignorant

13 **articulate**
  1 prepare carefully
  2 express clearly
  3 divide equally
  4 undertake eagerly

14 **buckle**
  1 roughen
  2 shake
  3 bend
  4 scorch

15 **assert**
  1 regret
  2 declare
  3 endure
  4 escape

16 **verbatim**
  1 in writing
  2 with explanation
  3 as a summary
  4 word for word

17 **civility**
1 cleverness
2 mercy
3 obedience
4 politeness

18 **hypothesis**
1 accepted policy
2 logical conclusion
3 tentative assumption
4 firm principle

19 **intrepid**
1 honorable
2 experienced
3 sensitive
4 brave

20 **leniently**
1 mildly
2 cautiously
3 successfully
4 thoughtfully

21 The report was very **concise**.
1 unusual
2 brief
3 scholarly
4 important

22 Her **adversary** was quite self-confident.
1 guide
2 attorney
3 opponent
4 subordinate

23 The agreement remained **intact** despite the situation.
1 acceptable
2 influential
3 productive
4 untouched

24 The worker **adamantly** refused to obey instructions.
1 generally
2 rarely
3 stubbornly
4 angrily

25 A verbal agreement **constituted** the contract between the partners.

1 formed
2 altered
3 refined
4 canceled

26 The office of the corporate president reflected great **affluence**.

1 taste
2 individuality
3 disorder
4 prosperity

27 The new senator **exploited** his political power.

1 took advantage of
2 tried out
3 clung to
4 bragged loudly about

28 He could not be **coerced** into taking action.

1 tricked
2 shamed
3 forced
4 bribed

29 She was given an award for being the most **congenial** participant in the contest.

1 talented
2 friendly
3 beautiful
4 clever

30 The negotiators worked **fruitlessly** toward their objective.

1 impatiently
2 half-heartedly
3 unsuccessfully
4 painfully

SPELLING

Directions (31–41): In each of the following groups of words, only one of the words is misspelled. In *each* group, select the misspelled word and spell it correctly in the space provided. [5]

_____ 31 countrys
injurious
camouflage
seizure
formulas

_____ 32 prevalent
irregular
accelaration
retail
judicious

_____ 33 unnecessary
misunderstand
silhouette
acquired
happyness

_____ 34 bachelor
accumulated
fuchsia
challanging
piloted

_____ 35 underneath
retreive
hereditary
undesirable
congratulatory

_____ 36 totality
explanation
occurred
forgotten
pianoes

_____ 37 unneeded
diseased
commited
tangible
perceived

_____ 38 disturbance
aweful
allotted
dissimilar
calendar

_____ 39 cylinder
conceivably
barely
dissappointed
scissors

_____ 40 arguement
harmonious
witness
performance
academy

READING COMPREHENSION

Directions (41–60): Below each of the following passages, there are several incomplete statements or questions about the passage. For each, select the word or expression that best completes the statement or answers the question in accordance with the meaning of the passage, and write its number in the space provided on the answer sheet. [20]

Passage A

In March 1943 I was sent by the Navy to a small town in north Texas. I was to begin learning to fly there — not at a proper naval establishment but at a civilian flying school. It wasn't much of a school: its staff was a couple of local crop-dusters, and its airport was a pasture on the edge of town, which we shared with the sheep.
5   It had no runway, only grass, which the sheep kept trimmed. It was not even flat — it sank in the middle, and rose steeply at the far side, where it ended in a grove of scrubby trees. At the corner of the field by the road was a small hangar, and a shed that was called the Flight Office; beside the hangar four or five Piper Cubs were parked. That was all the equipment there was, except for a windsock, once red and
10   yellow but faded now to an almost invisible gray, which drooped on a staff near the fence. There was nothing impressive or even substantial-looking about the place; but I took my first flight there, and soloed there, and I have the same sort of blurred affection for it that I have for other beginnings — for the first date, the first car, the first job.

15   First flight: what images remain? I am in the rear seat of a Cub, and my instructor is taxiing to the takeoff position. The wheels of the plane are small, and it rides very low, so that I seem to be sitting almost on the ground, and I feel every bump and hollow of the field as we taxi. The wings flap with the bumps, and the whole machine seems too small, too fragile, too casually put together to be trusted.

20   The instructor turns into the wind and runs up the engine, and I feel the quick lift of the plane. It begins to roll, bumpily at first, as though we are still taxiing. The nose is high, I can't see around it, and I have a panicky feeling that we are rushing toward something—a tree or a sheep or another plane; and then the flow of air begins to lift the wings, the tail comes up, and the plane moves with a new grace,
25   dancing, touching the rough field lightly, and then not touching it, skimming the grass, which is still so close that I can see each blade, and I am flying, lifted and carried by the streaming air.

At the end of the field the grove of trees is first a wall, a dark limit; and then it sinks and slides, foreshortening to a green island passing below us; the plane banks,
30 and I can see the town—but below me, all roofs and treetops—and beyond it there is distance, more and more distance, blue-hazy and flat and empty stretching away to the indistinct remote horizon. The world is enormous: the size of the earth increases around me, and so does the size of the air; space expands, is a tall dome filled with a pale clean light, into which we are climbing.

35   Below me the houses, each in its own place, look small and vulnerable perched on the largeness of the earth. I stare down at first like a voyeur, looking into other people's lives. A truck drives along a road and turns into a yard; a woman is hanging out clothes; she stops and runs to the truck. Should I be watching? Does she feel me there above her life? The world below exposes itself to me — I am flying,
40   I can see everything!

        – Samuel Hynes

41 The narrator suggests that he learned to fly in order to
   1 respond to parental pressure
   2 satisfy youthful curiosity
   3 fulfill military orders
   4 achieve a childhood dream

42 In lines 12 and 13, the expression "blurred affection" suggests a feeling of
   1 nostalgia   3 inspiration
   2 anger   4 depression

43 What is the meaning of the question "what images remain?" (line 15)?
   1 How much of the old airport is still there?
   2 What do I remember about the fight?
   3 What is the point of looking back?
   4 Was it real, or did I imagine it?

44 In the second paragraph, the description of the plane conveys the narrator's feelings of
   1 humility   3 frustration
   2 admiration   4 anxiety

45 In lines 30 through 34, the description conveys an impression of
   1 infinite space   3 dizzying height
   2 blinding speed   4 brilliant light

46 In lines 36 and 37, the narrator implies that a "voyeur" is someone who
1 threatens   3 snoops
2 flies   4 chases

47 In lines 39 and 40, the phrase "I am flying, I can see everything!" implies a sense of
1 defiance   3 contempt
2 thoughtfulness   4 exhilaration

Passage B

Rain

Old-timers are saying it's never
been so dry, but one of them disagrees,
remembering a drought so bad you could cross
the San Juan River downtown in your dress
5 oxfords and never get them wet.
I dream, at dawn, the rustle
of wind through leaves of aspen
and scrub oak into rain drumming
on the roof, dripping from the eaves,
10 the quilt covering my head into grey skies,
mist like a cool hand on my forehead.
Awakening, I scan the stony, turquoise
sky for clouds, interstices to crack
the blank days of endless blue.
15 Earth as dust, an unnerving heat at 2 PM
high in the mountains, the hot,
dry wind blowing grit in the teeth.
I want to beat my fists in the dusty
road, a sob in the throat. What if
20 it's our fault? Stripped of the comfort
of other droughts, cyclical, caused by
the world we're part of, have we
brought this one on ourselves? Scorching
the earth's deep green, burning
25 the sky a risk we took and lost?
We did all this and now: there's nothing
we can do to make it rain.

     — Holly St. John Bergon

48 In lines 6 through 9, the dream of rain is triggered by the
  1 pattering of squirrels on the roof
  2 sound of the wind in the trees
  3 greyness of the sky at dawn
  4 coolness of the night air

49 In lines 12 through 14, the words "stony," "blank," and "endless" suggest the
  1 silent acceptance of fate
  2 slow passage of time
  3 uneventfulness of the day
  4 relentlessness of the drought

50 In lines 18 and 19, the narrator expresses feelings of
  1 exhaustion
  2 hostility
  3 despair
  4 terror

51 In line 20, the poet suggests that the "comfort" of other droughts is the knowledge that
  1 other droughts did no harm
  2 people used to welcome the variety in weather
  3 people used to prefer dry weather
  4 other droughts were part of nature's pattern

52 What emotion is conveyed in lines 19 through 25?
  1 awe   3 resignation
  2 guilt   4 scorn

53 In lines 26 and 27, the narrator is concerned with the idea of the
  1 limitations of human power
  2 inevitability of drought
  3 vulnerability of human beings
  4 universality of suffering

54 What is ironic about the poem?
   1 It is set in the present but refers to the past.
   2 It asks questions but never answers them.
   3 It uses description but avoids comparison.
   4 Its title is "Rain" but is about drought.

Passage C

The first impressions one has of William Randolph Hearst's kingdom are not actually of his buildings (almost too overwhelming to enter right away) but of the elaborate, statue-strewn marginalia surrounding them. Hearst never saw a rose garden that he did not think would be improved by a marble statue of Europa gal-
5 loping bare-bottomed on a bull through it. And after seeing Hearst's swimming pools you realize, humbly, that you have never really seen a swimming pool before.

The Neptune Pool is built on a promontory overlooking the Pacific, a huge oval tank holding some 350,000 gallons of water, surrounded by concentric circles of Greco-Roman marble columns, a nice place to shoot a new movie version of "Julius Caesar."
10 But the indoor pool beneath the tennis courts (which have glass skylights along the net lines to provide interior lighting) is even more spectacular. The pool is entirely surrounded by gold-leaf and blue mosaic tiles that are also set into the walls and ceilings to double their image in the water. Electrified alabaster lamps bloom along the pool's edge where swimmers once climbed in and out on carved marble ladders.
15 But by now, the visitor accepts carved marble swimming pool ladders as being both reasonable and even necessary. We have mentally quickened our stride to keep up with Hearst's appetites, income and audacity. This is someone who ordered more than one ancient oak tree (whose branches covered a complete acre with
20 shade) uprooted and replanted. When he died, an entire Spanish monastery lay in a warehouse, in individual stones waiting to be reassembled.

Hearst in his lifetime ran newspapers, sat briefly in Congress, was held responsible in the main for starting the Spanish-American War, tried to become President and was seemingly everywhere in the country at once, inspiring fear, hatred and
25 loyalty. (As his columnist Ambrose Bierce once wrote, "Nobody but God loves him and he knows it.") But there never seemed to be a day in Hearst's life when he did not also buy something, once jotting "I'll take everything — WRH" on the top of an art dealer's catalogue. Hearst was a compulsive shopper and all the world was his mall.

— Phyllis Theroux

55 According to the passage, a visitor to Hearst's estate is first impressed by the
   1 beauty of the buildings
   2 ornateness of the grounds
   3 tranquility of the setting
   4 number of swimming pools

56 In lines 3 through 5, the reference to a garden and statue
    has the effect of
    1 celebrating Hearst's knowledge of flowers
    2 explaining Hearst's source of wealth
    3 suggesting Hearst's love of animals
    4 ridiculing Hearst's use of statues

57 In line 11, the author states that the indoor pool "is even
    more spectacular" than the
    1 Neptune Pool   3 tennis courts
    2 Pacific   4 skylights

58 In lines 20 and 21, the reference to the monastery implies
    that Hearst had
    1 bought the monastery
    2 destroyed the monastery
    3 become religious
    4 lost interest in swimming pools

59 The effect of lines 22 through 25 is to
    1 highlight Hearst's constant success
    2 reveal Hearst's lack of a personal life
    3 list Heart's varied experiences
    4 demonstrate Hearst's drive for perfection

60 The anecdote about the art catalogue illustrates Hearst's
    1 good taste   3 knowledge
    2 busy schedule   4 extravagance

PART 2

Directions: Write a well-organized essay of about 250 words on
either *A* or *B*. [25]

A In some works of literature, an individual's behavior is the
   result of being troubled by an event or situation from the

past. From the literature you have read, choose *two* works in which an individual's behavior is a result of being troubled by the past. For *each* work, identify the individual and describe the event or situation from the past that troubles the individual. Using specific references from *each* work, tell how the individual's behavior is affected by the troubling event or situation. Give titles and authors.

B Although some characters in literature serve an important function because they change, others serve an important function because they do not change. From the literature you have read, choose *two* works in which a character does not change but still serves an important function. For *each* work, identify the character. Using specific references from *each* work, discuss the character's function in the work and explain the significance of having this character remain the same throughout the work. Give titles and authors.

PART 3

Directions: Answer A <u>or</u> B <u>or</u> C. [30]

A Your school is going to hire a new principal. You are a member of the committee that will be interviewing candidates for this position. The committee chairperson has asked each member to identify one school-related issue each candidate should address in the interview. In a letter of about 250 words to the committee chairperson, identify the issue that you want the candidate to address and explain why you think the issue is important. Use specific reasons, examples, or details. *Write only the body of the letter.*

B You have been invited to be a guest writer for the music column of your local newspaper and have decided to use this opportunity to introduce your readers to music that you feel should have a wider audience. Choose two musical works that you believe should have a wider audience.

In an article of about 250 words for your local newspaper, identify the two musical works and discuss the elements that make each work worthy of having a wider audience. Use specific reasons, examples, or details.

C Write a well-organized composition of about 250 words on one of the following topics:

Big city/small neighborhood	The parent I hope to be
Life without television	A matter of trust
Danger: second-hand smoke	Hometown teams

ANSWER KEY
PRACTICE EXAM ONE

Part 1

1.	4	21.	2	41.	3
2.	3	22.	3	42.	1
3.	3	23.	4	43.	2
4.	2	24.	3	44.	4
5.	1	25.	1	45.	1
6.	4	26.	4	46.	3
7.	3	27.	1	47.	4
8.	2	28.	3	48.	2
9.	1	29.	2	49.	4
10.	4	30.	3	50.	3
11.	2	31.	countries	51.	4
12.	1	32.	acceleration	52.	2
13.	2	33.	happiness	53.	1
14.	3	34.	challenging	54.	4
15.	2	35.	retrieve	55.	2
16.	4	36.	pianos	56.	4
17.	4	37.	committed	57.	1
18.	3	38.	awful	58.	1
19.	4	39.	disappointed	59.	3
20.	1	40.	argument	60.	4

ANSWERS AND EXPLANATIONS
PRACTICE EXAM ONE

PART 1
Reading Comprehension

1. **4**

   1 The editor doesn't appear until many lines later.

   2 Woolf doesn't say anything about a lack of competition.

   3 Woolf doesn't mention friends.

   4 **Correct.** In her second sentence, Woolf says, "Many . . . women . . . have been before me, making the path smooth, and regulating my steps."

2. **3**

   1 There's no mention yet of generating income.

   2 Fame has not been mentioned.

   3 **Correct.** Writing was "harmless." "The family peace was not broken . . . No demand was made upon the family purse."

   4 There's no mention of entertainment.

3. **3**

   1 "But to tell you my story—it is a simple one. You have only got to imagine a girl in a bedroom with a pen in her hand." She says it's *her* story. This implies that the girl was she.

   2 "But to tell you my story—it is a simple one. You have only got to imagine a girl in a bedroom with a pen in her hand." She says it's *her* story, which implies that the girl was she.

   3 **Correct.** "But to tell you my story—it is a simple one. You have only got to imagine a girl in a bedroom with a pen in her hand." She says it's *her* story, which implies that the girl was she.

   4 She does say "you have only got to imagine," but she clearly implies that the girl is she, not someone imaginary.

4. **2**

  1 We never hear that an editor offered her a job.

  2 **Correct.** She says that she slipped a few pages into an envelope and the envelope into a mailbox and "It was thus I became a journalist[.]"

  3 She never says she applied for a position.

  4 No friend is mentioned.

5. **1**

  1 **Correct.** Woolf says "Articles have to be about something. Mine . . . was about a novel by a famous man. And while I was writing this review. . . ." So her early writings were book reviews.

  2 No poems are mentioned.

  3 Woolf mentions a novel by a famous man, not by her.

  4 No mystery stories are mentioned.

6. **4**

  1 Woolf describes the Angel as sympathetic, charming, unselfish, pure, and always putting others before herself. There is no mention of honest.

  2 Woolf describes the Angel as sympathetic, charming, unselfish, pure, and always putting others before herself. There is no mention of self-reliant.

  3 Woolf describes the Angel as sympathetic, charming, unselfish, pure, and always putting others before herself. There is no mention of inquisitive.

  4 **Correct.** Yes. Woolf describes the Angel as sympathetic, charming, unselfish, pure, and always putting others before herself. That's self-sacrificing.

7. **3**

  1 Common sense tells you that "pure" does not necessarily mean young.

  2 Common sense tells you that "pure" does not mean frivolous.

3 **Correct.** "Pure" is used to mean she never did anything wrong; she was virtuous.

4 "Pure" here does not mean plain. Being plain would mean the Angel was unattractive, and there's no sense of that here.

8.   2

1 This question is too difficult, but you can eliminate "status" because it has nothing to do with the passage.

2 **Correct.** "Integrity" is used here to mean "wholeness." Woolf says that the Angel would have killed her, but because the Angel is a phantom, you know that she could not have *physically* killed Woolf, so Woolf is implying that listening to this part of herself would have torn her apart.

3 This is a perfectly good guess, but Woolf doesn't say the Angel would have driven her insane. She says that the Angel would have killed her, so "integrity" is the answer.

4 Eliminate "history" because it has nothing to do with the passage.

9.   1

1 **Correct.** The whole passage is about how the Angel tormented Woolf and kept her from writing. That's an obstacle.

2 The Angel could be seen as a traitor to Woolf, but this is stretching a little.

3 She may have some characteristics of a flirt, but "obstacle" is a better answer.

4 Woolf does not describe the Angel as cowardly.

10.   4

1 A muse is someone or something that inspires you to be creative, not someone or something that prevents you from being creative.

2 She is not the spirit of other *writers*; she prevents women from writing.

3 There is no indication of death.

4 **Correct.** The Angel symbolizes to Woolf the ideal woman of that time, who was not a writer or anyone who had her own ideas.

Vocabulary

11. 2 What do athletes do when they get product endorsements? They say they really like the sneakers, car, or whatever. So, the best guess is choice 2, "approval."

12. 1 What happens when metal corrodes? It wears away gradually. So, something corrosive must wear things away gradually, which leads you right to choice 1.

13. 2 In this case, *articulate* is being used as a verb, meaning "to express clearly." If you mumble, your teacher may ask you to articulate your words so that he or she can understand you. You may have heard someone being described as articulate, meaning that person speaks well.

14. 3 In this case, we're not talking about the buckle of a belt but rather another meaning of buckle, the verb *to buckle*, as in "to buckle under the pressure." That means "to bend."

15. 2 Somewhere along the line, you've no doubt heard someone say, "Assert yourself." Even if you don't know what that means, "endure yourself," "regret yourself," and "escape yourself" don't make sense, do they?

16. 4 The *verb-* in *verbatim* should remind you of *verbal*. *Verbal* means "having to do with words," so go with the only answer choice that mentions words directly, choice 4.

17. 4 What does it mean when someone is very civilized? It means that he or she is polite. From this you can infer that *civility* is "politeness."

18. 3   You've seen this word before in your chemistry and physics classes. Think back. It's an idea that you think is true but that still must be tested to be proved.

19. 4   Have you ever heard of the Navy ship the *Intrepid*? Is the Navy going to call one of its ships the *Sensitive*? How about the *Experiences*? The answer is no on both counts, so you can eliminate choices 2 and 3.

20. 1   You may have heard a teacher say, "If you forget your homework once, I'll be lenient, but after that you'll get a zero." To be *lenient* means to be "tolerant or mild, not severe."

21. 2   It's the rare student who can make it through high school without being told to make his or her writing more concise. What does that mean? It means "keep it brief."

22. 3   An adverse reaction is a bad reaction. So, *adversary* must also be a negative word. Lose choices 1, 2, and 4.

23. 4   *Intact* means "whole," so choice 4 comes closest.

24. 3   If you're adamant, you don't budge, so the answer is 3, "stubbornly."

25. 1   *Constituted* should remind you of the word *Constitution*. Use this as you go through the answer choices. Did the Constitution form something? Yes, abso-

lutely. Did it alter, refine, or cancel anything? No, so the answer must be choice 1, "formed."

26. 4   Even if you don't know that affluence is wealth, consider whether a corporate president's office is likely to reflect disorder or free-spirited individuality. This should prompt you to eliminate choices 2 and 3.

27. 1   *Exploit* means "to use to one's advantage."

28. 3   To coerce is to force someone to do something.

29. 2   If you break *congenial* down, you get the prefix *con-*, which means "with," and *genial*, which means "friendly." This leads you directly to answer choice 2.

30. 3   You probably know that *fruitful* means "successful." So, you can guess that *fruitlessly* means "unsuccessfully."

Spelling

31. countries

32. acceleration

33. happiness

34. challenging

35. retrieve

36. pianos

37. committed

38. awful

39. disappointed

40. argument

Reading Comprehension

41. 3

   1 Where do you see anything about parents?

   2 There is no mention of youthful curiosity.

   3 **Correct.** In the first line, the narrator says that he was "sent by the Navy" to learn to fly. From this, we can assume that he learned to fly to fulfill military orders.

   4 Don't get all romantic! He never says anything about a childhood dream.

42. 1

   1 **Correct.** Nostalgia is a sentimental and affectionate memory of the past. The author's "blurred affection" for the flying school definitely qualifies.

   2 Before you even go back to the passage, the term "blurred affection" tells you that you need an answer choice that's positive, so anger is out.

   3 The narrator never says anything about inspiration.

   4 The author feels a "blurred affection"—in other words, something positive. Depression is negative. Lose it.

43. **2**

1 How does the narrator answer the question? He doesn't do it with speculations about how much of the airport is still around. Therefore, lose this choice.

2 **Correct.** Read a few lines after the question "what images remain?" The narrator describes his memories of his first flight. So, we can assume that the question means, "What do I remember about the flight?"

3 Does the narrator follow his question with a discussion of the pointlessness of looking back? As he doesn't, this couldn't be what the question means.

4 Does the narrator answer the question "what images remain?" with a musing on reality versus fantasy? No, so that couldn't be what the question is about.

44. **4**

1 Humility is the state of being humble. In this paragraph, the narrator's too busy feeling stressed to have time for humility.

2 The author describes the plane as "too small, too fragile, too casually put together to be trusted" (line 19). That definitely doesn't sound like admiration.

3 There's nothing in the paragraph to suggest that the narrator is feeling frustration.

4 **Correct.** The author says that the plane was "too small, too fragile, too casually put together to be trusted" (line 19). He's definitely feeling anxious and, from the sound of things, rightly so.

45. **1**

1 **Correct.** The narrator keeps talking about "distance, more and more distance" (line 31). Infinite space is an excellent paraphrase of this.

2 Focus! Speed is not mentioned in these lines.

3 The narrator talks about space in these lines but doesn't dwell on his height above the ground.

4 The only mention of light in this section is of "pale clean light" (line 34). This is not the same as brilliant light.

46. 3

   1 Is the author threatening anyone in these lines? No, he's just looking.

   2 Yes, he's flying, but that's not the point here. In these lines, he describes himself as "a voyeur, looking into other people's lives" (lines 36–37). A voyeur isn't someone who flies; it's someone who snoops.

   3 **Correct.** Read the whole sentence: The narrator describes himself as "a voyeur, looking into other people's lives" (lines 36–37); in other words, he's snooping.

   4 The author isn't chasing anyone in these lines. He's just "looking into other people's lives" (lines 36–37).

47. 4

   1 Defiance? Who's he defying? He's just happy and excited.

   2 Thoughtfulness is a state of quiet, calm thinking. In these lines, the narrator is too excited for that.

   3 Even if you don't know that *contempt* means "loathing and disgust," you probably do know that it's a negative word. Because the narrator is clearly having a rocking good time in these lines, you can eliminate this answer choice.

   4 **Correct.** In these lines, the author clearly is getting a rush out of flying. That's exhilaration.

48. 2

   1 Squirrels? Where do you see anything about squirrels in these lines?

   2 **Correct.** The narrator talks about "the rustle/of wind through leaves" (lines 6–7). That's an excellent paraphrase of the sound of the wind in the trees.

   3 There's nothing about grey skies until line 10.

   4 There's nothing here about cool air.

49. 4

   1 Is the narrator accepting her fate? No, she's searching the sky for rain clouds that would end the drought.

   2 There's nothing in these lines to suggest that time is passing slowly.

3 The narrator isn't describing one particular day in these lines: She's describing all of the days of the drought.

4 **Correct.** "Stony," "blank," and "endless" describe what things are like during the drought: unchanging and showing no signs of getting better.

50. 3

1 If she's beating her fists in the road, she must have some energy left, so exhausted is not the best choice.

2 *Hostile* means "very unfriendly." That's not quite what's going on in these lines.

3 **Correct.** Beating her fists in the road and sobbing sounds closer to despair than to any of the other answer choices.

4 The "sob in the throat" (line 19) sounds like it could be about terror, but the fist-beating definitely does not. Because this answer choice is only half good, lose it.

51. 4

1 Use common sense to eliminate this one: We know that droughts cause harm.

2 Do you believe that people used to welcome droughts and other natural calamities? This is not likely.

3 "Gosh, this drought sure is a drag, but at least we can take comfort in the fact that people used to hate humidity." Does this make any sense? No; eliminate it.

4 **Correct.** This is a good paraphrase of "other droughts, cyclical, caused by / the world we're part of" (lines 21–22).

52. 2

1 *Awe* is a positive word. The narrator is not expressing anything positive in these lines.

2 **Correct.** The first sentence of this section tips you off: "What if / it's our fault?" (lines 19–20). And later, "have we / brought this one on ourselves?" (lines 22–23). The narrator is totally consumed with guilt.

3 Resignation is calm acceptance of something bad. The author is certainly not calm in these lines.

4 Scorn is angry rejection or dismissal. The author is definitely not being scornful of the drought in these lines.

53.   1

1 **Correct.** The phrase "there's nothing/we can do" (lines 26–27) tips you off that the narrator is thinking about humans' limitations.

2 These lines are not about the drought itself but about humans' inability to make it go away.

3 This answer is close but not quite right. These lines are not as much about humans' vulnerability as they are about humans' inability to control nature.

4 The universality of suffering means the idea that everyone, everywhere suffers. This idea doesn't come up in these lines or, for that matter, anywhere else in the poem.

54.   4

1 Irony is the use of a word or phrase to express its opposite. There's nothing ironic here about remembering the past.

2 Annoying, yes; ironic, no. Irony is the use of a word or phrase to express its opposite.

3 Irony is the use of a word or phrase to express its opposite. There's nothing ironic about using or not using description or comparison.

4 **Correct.** Irony is the use of a word or phrase to express its opposite. The poem is called "Rain" but is about a lack of rain. Irony, pure and simple.

55.   2

1 Be careful. In the first two lines, the author says that the "first impressions . . . are not actually of his buildings."

2 **Correct.** This first sentence gets a little twisty, but the author finally says that the visitor is first impressed by the "elaborate, statue-strewn marginalia" surrounding [the buildings]" (line 3). Even if you don't know what marginalia is, you do know that *ornate* is a good paraphrase for "elaborate" and that the grounds are the land surrounding the buildings.

3 The place that the author describes in the first paragraph sounds anything but tranquil (that is, calm and peaceful).

4 In line 3, the author says that the visitor is first impressed by the "elaborate, statue-strewn marginalia" surrounding [the buildings]." You may not know what marginalia is, but you can guess that the swimming pools would not be "statue-strewn" and "surrounding [the buildings]," so you can eliminate this answer choice.

56. 4

1 The author never says that Hearst knew anything about flowers, just that he overdecorated his flower gardens with statues.

2 There's no mention in these lines of Hearst's source of wealth.

3 Love of animals? Just because in the statue, the naked lady is riding on a bull? That's a bit of a stretch.

4 **Correct.** These lines are poking fun at Hearst's love of excess: He's got to drop a statue of a naked lady in the middle of every garden.

57. 1

1 **Correct.** First, the author describes the Neptune Pool. Then, he describes the indoor pool as "even more spectacular." These lines are a little confusing, because they are all one long, messy sentence. Even if you get completely lost, though, this is the best guess: The most logical thing with which to compare one pool is another pool.

2 It's easy to get confused here, because the sentence structure gets very complicated. The Pacific is mentioned only as something you can see from the Neptune Pool.

3 The author says that the indoor pool is beneath the tennis courts, but she doesn't ever compare the two.

4 The skylights are just part of the tennis court. Don't get confused because they are the last things the author mentions before she starts talking about the indoor pool.

58. 1

1 **Correct.** The author suggests that Hearst bought the monastery with the idea of having it taken apart, and then he put back together again at a more convenient (for him) location.

2 We know that Hearst planned to have the monastery reassembled, but we don't know who took it apart in the first place.

3 Be careful not to make assumptions. All we really know is that he liked to buy things.

4 What, can't a guy be interested in monasteries and swimming pools at the same time?

59. **3**

1 Starting a war and losing a race for the presidency: Even his own mother couldn't call that constant success.

2 These lines say nothing about Hearst's personal life. For all we know, he was a party animal in his spare time.

3 **Correct.** That's just what these lines do: They tell what Hearst did with himself when he wasn't having swimming pools built.

4 There's nothing in these lines about a drive for perfection.

60. **4**

1 Do we know that everything in the catalogue was tasteful? No, so we don't know whether Hearst's desire to buy everything in it shows that he had good taste.

2 This is being a bit too kind. From this anecdote, we know nothing about the guy's schedule. We just know that he bought everything he could get his hands on.

3 Do we know that everything in the catalogue was good or valuable? No, so we don't know what buying everything in the catalogue says about Hearst's knowledge.

4 **Correct.** Could he really have *needed* everything in the art dealer's catalogue? I think not. That's extravagance, pure and simple.

Part 2

Essay A

Score: 88 percent

In many works of literature, characters behave in a way that reflects their unease over an event from the past. In Toni Morrison's *Beloved*, for example, Sethe is literally haunted by the ghost of the baby daughter who she killed. In Tennessee Williams' *A Streetcar Named Desire*, Blanche can't get over the deaths of her husband and relatives, and that she has ended up in poverty.

In *Beloved*, Sethe kills her infant daughter Beloved so that the baby will not become a slave. Soon after, Beloved reappears, first as a ghostly presence, and then, eighteen years after her death, in the form of a seemingly real young girl hungry for Sethe's love and attention. Sethe takes in this girl who appears from nowhere and although Beloved is bizarre, whiny and demanding, using up both Sethe's energy and her daughter Denver's, Sethe continually loves her and cares for her. Sethe has never recovered from the trauma of killing her daughter and now that this girl needs her she feels that in some way she is making up for what happened by mothering this girl. Beloved torments Sethe with painful questions about her past and one day even seems to try to strangle Sethe. In return, Sethe treats Beloved better than her own daughter Denver, giving Beloved two skates when they go ice-skating, while Sethe and Denver share a pair. In every way, Sethe's treatment of Beloved is a way to try to recover from the trauma of killing her daughter.

Blanche, the faded Southern belle in *A Streetcar Named Desire*, behaves throughout in a way that is inappropriately flirtatious, especially toward the neighbor, Mitch, but even toward her sister's husband, Stanley. The first time Blanche meets Stanley she asks him to help her button her dress. Blanche also lies to Mitch about her past, showing herself as wholesome and girlish when in reality she has been promiscuous and now has a bad reputation in her small town. We eventually learn, however, that Blanche's actions come from a horrible string of events in her past, including her young husband's suicide, which Blanche feels responsible for. Blanche recounts that after discovering her husband with another man, Blanche had told him she was disgusted by him and immediately afterwards he shot himself. Blanche also tells of being alone with several family members at their deaths. She reveals that she is behaving the way she does now to try to block out the memory of all the death she has seen.

Both Sethe and Blanche have suffered through terrible tragedies, and, not surprisingly, these tragedies affect their behavior significantly. Each character, in her own way, does what she can to recover from the pain she has experienced.

Comments

This essay is quite strong and demonstrates a thorough understanding of the question. The Streetcar paragraph could be organized a little better, maybe by starting with a topic sentence that clearly explains that Blanche is blocking out troubling events from her past. It takes a bit too long for the paragraph to address that point as it stands right now.

Part 3

Composition C

Score: 83 percent

The Parent I Hope to Be

I baby-sit for a four-year-old girl named Sofia who is so cute that people come up to whoever she's with to tell him or her how beautiful Sofia is. When she's with her mother and people tell her how beautiful she is, her mother always says "and smart and strong!" Now Sofia says it too. Someone tells her she's adorable, or cute, or beautiful, and Sofia declares "and smart and strong!" I've watched this happen and I've decided that this is the kind of parent I want to be—one who does whatever she can to make sure her children feel that they are capable of anything.

It will be a long time before I have children but I already watch my parents and my friends' parents and identify the things they do that I want to imitate and the things that I want to remember never to do. I think the most important thing to do is to encourage your kids to be themselves and to have faith in their decisions. Too many parents second-guess their kids' decisions and try to make their kids do what the parents think is best. One boy I know is starting college next year and is going to major in pre-med because his parents want him to be a doctor. He doesn't want to be a doctor; he wants to coach sports, or teach physical education, or something like that. His parents know this, but have decided that what he is interested in is not important and somehow it will be better if he becomes a doctor. Can't his parents see that he'll never be happy that way? They are giving him the message that he can't make the right decision by himself and they have to make it for him.

Children learn from observing their parents, and parents send messages to their children even without trying to. I know that the way I live my life will send messages to my children. Therefore, it is my responsibility to live my life the way I want my children to live theirs. If I want my children to have faith in themselves, I need to show the same faith in myself. That is what I must work towards in the years before I have children, so that I can be the parent I hope to be.

Comments

The essay's introduction is strong and the "smart and strong" quote is effective. The essay would be improved if the author had used the quote again later—perhaps in the conclusion—to tie the points together. In the second paragraph the word "your" should be removed from the phrase "encourage your kids." The transition from the second paragraph to the conclusion is choppy, as the conclusion seems to start a new idea and never returns to the original point.

PRACTICE EXAM TWO

PART 1

READING COMPREHENSION

The following passage describes the Norman conquest of the Saxons at the Battle of Hastings in 1066. The passage is adapted from the PBS television series *Connections* by James Burke.

At dawn on a bitterly cold day—Friday, October 13, 1066—Harold, Saxon King of England, and his exhausted army finally pushed their way through the last few miles of dense forest that covered most of southeast England. Harold and his men had marched to the village of Hastings straight from their battle with the Danes at Lincolnshire, 270 miles to the north, in the quite extraordinary time of ten days. To make up for their losses at the battle they had gathered levies of men from the counties they passed through on their way south. Even so, Harold arrived at the ridge above Hastings with only a remnant of the host of men he had taken against the Danes two weeks before. He may have had at most five thousand trained fighting men. Many of these would have carried the iron-tipped ash spear, or a throwing axe, and a sword; some were bowmen, most wore leather caps and very few had mail shirts. Ranged alongside these professionals were the levies: farmers and peasants, for the most part, who had been straggling in from all over the southern countries during the previous few days.

Against this motley group stood the troops of Duke William of Normandy, later to be known as the Conqueror. The Normans had landed sixteen days before and had had over two weeks in which to rest and prepare for battle with Harold. William had over eight thousand fully trained fighters, including 1000 archers and 3000 cavalry. All of them were both well fed and well trained. They used standard weapons—lances, spears, axes, bows and arrows, swords—and most of them wore steel caps and mails shirts.

During the night of the thirteenth William offered terms: he would rule the south, and Harold could retain everything north of the river Humber. After some discussion in the Saxon camp Harold refused the offer, and battle was inevitable. Although Harold was unaware of the fact, he had already lost. For in the ensuing battle the Normans were to use a devise of crucial significance that had been perfected in northern France over the previous hundred years. Harold and his predecessors knew of its existence, and indeed used it themselves, but the conservative fighting style of the Saxons may have prevented them from realizing its full potential.

As the battle began, King Harold's Saxon army was grouped along the top of the ridge, along a front stretching for 800 yards. The trained men stood at the front, looking across at the Normans on a slight rise to the south. In the cold light of that October morning, the Saxons shuffled into position so that the shield wall stretched unbroken along the length of the front. The shield wall had been the standard defensive tactic used by the foot soldier against cavalry since late Roman times. Harold's men were on foot because that is the way they had always fought. To ride a horse into battle would have been to come to the field already prepared to fight, and such was against the Saxon battle ethic, which decreed that if a man's lord died on the field, he could not leave it alive. So what use was a horse? Behind the front line came the levies, the farmers with their billhooks, hammers, and pitchforks.

At 9 a.m. the Normans advanced under a hail of arrows from their bow-men. The plan was to break the Saxon line down with the arrow strike, and cut into it with the cavalry as the arrows took their toll. It failed. The Normans advanced up the hill towards the shield wall, and were beaten back with an avalanche of spears and axes. Again the Normans tried to ride through the shield wall, but fell back exhausted, after battering at it for more than two hours. As the Normans retreated into the valley the Saxons made their great mistake. They broke ranks and followed the Normans down to level ground. At that moment the Norman cavalry turned and, standing in their stirrups, cut the Saxons to pieces beneath their horses' feet. Here, where the ground was flat, the Norman cavalry shock-troop went through the English mass like a hot knife through butter. It was William's use of the stirrup to build a shock-troop of cavalry that gave him the ability to ride down the Saxons once they were on level ground. Twenty of the Normans charged King Harold's royal banner at the top of the ridge. In the desperate, hand-to-hand slaughter that followed, Harold's bodyguards went down before him in true Saxon tradition, taking sixteen of the Normans with them. The four survivors attacked Harold and killed him. By 5 p.m. on October 14, 1066, England was Norman.

1 King Harold's soldiers were exhausted when they arrived at the battle site because they
 1 had climbed steep terrain
 2 had to take a roundabout route
 3 were wearing heavy armor
 4 were returning from another battle

2 Which statement best describes King Harold's army just prior to the battle?
 1 The army was as well trained as the enemy.
 2 The army was untested in battle.
 3 The army was greatly reduced in size.
 4 The army was fully equipped for battle.

3 The description of the Norman troops suggests that they
  1 objected to unnecessary waste
  2 had an advantage in the forthcoming battle
  3 were unable to wage inland war
  4 were eager to seize the hill

4 Who broke off the negotiations that could have prevented the battle?
  1 the Danish general   3 King Harold
  2 the peasant leaders   4 Duke William

5 To what does the speaker attribute the fact that the battle "was already lost"?
  1 an important invention
  2 superiority of numbers and weapons
  3 discord among the troops
  4 the placement of the opposing armies

6 At the beginning of the battle, which men occupied the front line of King Harold's army?
  1 expert archers   3 men on horseback
  2 armed peasants   4 trained soldiers

7 What did fighting on horseback represent to King Harold's lords?
  1 deception   3 nobility
  2 tradition   4 cowardice

8 What strategy did the Normans use to protect their advancing cavalry?
  1 a predawn attack   3 defensive camouflage
  2 an arrow strike   4 troop division

9 What tactical mistake did the Saxons make?
   1 They retreated under the shield wall.
   2 They left the front line weakened.
   3 They followed the retreating Normans.
   4 They hurled their weapons too early.

10 What was the "device of crucial significance" that con-
    tributed to the Norman victory?
   1 the stirrup   3 the shield
   2 the arrow   4 the spear

VOCABULARY

Directions (11–30): Choose the number of the word or phrase
that most nearly expresses the meaning of the word printed in
heavy black type. [10]

11 **compulsion**
   1 ongoing depression   3 strong impulse
   2 erratic pulse   4 deceptive calmness

12 **laden**
   1 optimistic   3 constant
   2 burdened   4 criminal

13 **unconditionally**
   1 absolutely   3 honestly
   2 voluntarily   4 knowingly

14 **dire**
   1 dreadful   3 disorganized
   2 unexplainable   4 embarrassing

15 **mandate**
   1 liberate   3 acknowledge
   2 abolish   4 command

16 **audacity**
   1 excitement
   2 expectation
   3 annoyance
   4 boldness

17 **reprieve**
   1 temporary relief
   2 appropriate punishment
   3 unlawful escape
   4 immediate revenge

18 **impeach**
   1 libel
   2 accuse
   3 defeat
   4 punish

19 **conversely**
   1 on the contrary
   2 as a matter of fact
   3 on the whole
   4 in addition to

20 **transpire**
   1 fade
   2 compromise
   3 occur
   4 hurry

21 The suspect **fabricated** the story.
   1 created
   2 ridiculed
   3 denied
   4 explained

22 According to the critics, the artist's work was **pedestrian**.
   1 ridiculous
   2 childish
   3 disturbing
   4 ordinary

23 The sailor waited **apprehensively** for news about his shipmates.
   1 with uneasiness
   2 with curiosity
   3 with boredom
   4 with grief

24 The professor voiced her opinion **emphatically**.
   1 reluctantly   3 forcefully
   2 diplomatically   4 immediately

25 The new supervisor worked hard to eliminate the workers' **tedium**.
   1 laziness   3 insecurity
   2 boredom   4 regret

26 The writer was asked to **append** a list of resources.
   1 explain   3 number
   2 summarize   4 attach

27 As a result of numerous accidents, the construction site was under **scrutiny**.
   1 careful examination   3 justifiable attack
   2 extensive repair   4 continuous patrol

28 The speaker's conclusion was **plausible**.
   1 clever   3 straightforward
   2 believable   4 troubling

29 The new administration wanted to **consolidate** several assistance programs.
   1 create   3 cancel
   2 change   4 combine

30 The architect proved to be **inept**.
   1 lazy   3 careless
   2 unfit   4 uninspired

Directions (31–40): In each of the following groups of words, only one of the words is misspelled. In each group, select the misspelled word and spell it correctly in the space provided. [5]

_____ 31 enrollment
grease
enliven
goalkeeper
qualafy

_____ 32 dissatisfied
whistle
abundant
ballet
intellectuel

_____ 33 antenna
cieling
controlled
disguise
physician

_____ 34 noticeable
nineteenth
definitely
conscioussness
renounce

_____ 35 enemies
incompetent
allergick
ecstasy
spaghetti

_____ 36 apology
calendar
unmistakable
salarys
preexisting

_____ 37 fierce
chaperoned
fragrence
rodeos
simultaneous

_____ 38 weird
truly
disappear
fullfill
assets

_____ 39 attendence
accuracy
manageable
license
unneeded

_____ 40 nuclear
vacination
actress
sacrifice
disapproval

READING COMPREHENSION

Directions (41–60): Below each of the following passages, there are several incomplete statements or questions about the passage. For each, select the word or expression that best completes the statement or answers the question in accordance with the meaning of the passage.[20]

Passage A

We weren't doing anything. We hadn't hurt anybody, and we didn't want to. We were on holiday. We had studied maps of the city and taken hundreds of photographs. We had walked ourselves dizzy and stared at the other visitors and stammered out our barely Berlitz versions of a beautiful language. We had mar-
5 veled at the convenient frequency of the Metro and devoured vegetarian crêpes from a sidewalk concession. Among ourselves, we extolled the seductive intelligence and sensual style of this Paris, this magical place to celebrate the two hundredth anniversary of the French Revolution, this obvious place to sit back with a good glass of wine and think about a world lit by longings for Liberty, Equality,
10 Fraternity.

It was raining. It was dark. It was late. We hurried along, punch-drunk with happiness and fatigue. Behind us, the Cathedral of the Sacred Heart glowed ivory and gorgeous in a flattering wash of artificial, mellow light.

These last hours of our last full day in Paris seemed to roll and slide into plea-
15 sure and surprise. I was happy. I was thinking that, as a matter of fact, the more things change, the more things change.

I was thinking that if we, all of us black, all of us women, all of us deriving from connected varieties of peasant/immigrant/persecuted histories of struggle and significant triumph, if we could find and trust each other enough to travel
20 together into a land where none of us belonged, nothing on Earth was impossible anymore.

But then we tried to get a cab to stop for us, and we failed. We tried again, and then again. One driver actually stopped and then, suddenly, he sped away, almost taking with him the arm of one of my companions who had been about to
25 open the door to his taxi.

This was a miserable conclusion to a day of so much tourist privilege and delight, a day of feeling powerful because to be a sightseer is to be completely welcome among strangers. And that's the trick of it: No one will say "no" to freely given admiration and respect. But now we had asked for something in return—a
30 taxi. And with that single, ordinary request, the problems of our identity, our problems of power, reappeared and trashed our holiday confidence and joy.

— June Jordan

41 The meaning of the phrase "barely Berlitz versions" (line 4) is enhanced by what other word?
1 "dizzy" (line 3)   3 "visitors" (line 3)
2 "stared" (line 3)   4 "stammered" (line 4)

42 According to lines 6 through 10, what does Paris symbolize for the narrator?
1 courage   3 romance
2 fashion   4 freedom

43 In the second paragraph, the narrator's description of the cathedral and its surroundings emphasizes the contrast between
1 sadness and cheer   3 light and dark
2 space and time   4 stability and change

44 In lines 17 through 21, the narrator expresses pleasure at her realization that she and her companions
1 had become best friends
2 could learn French so easily
3 could feel comfortable in a strange land
4 were celebrating an anniversary

45 In the fifth paragraph, what does the narrator imply about the cab drivers?
1 They were prejudiced.
2 They were reckless.
3 They were dishonest.
4 They were irresponsible.

46 Which statement best describes the narrator's feelings about her last hours in Paris?
1 She was perplexed.
2 She was frightened
3 She was disheartened.
4 She was angry.

47 The incident with the cab drivers was foreshadowed in which line or lines?

1 line 1 3 lines 14 and 15

2 lines 11 and 12 4 lines 17 and 18

Passage B
The Gift

To pull the metal splinter from my palm
my father recited a story in a low voice.
I watched his lovely face and not the blade.
Before the story ended he'd removed
5 the iron sliver I thought I'd die from.

I can't remember the tale
but hear his voice still, a well
of dark water, a prayer.
And I recall his hands,
10 two measures of tenderness
he laid against my face,
the flames of discipline
he raised above my head.

Had you entered that afternoon
15 you would have thought you saw a man
planting something in a boy's palm,
a silver tear, a tiny flame.
Had you followed that
you would have arrived here,
20 where I bend over my wife's right hand.

Look how I shave her thumbnail down
so carefully she feels no pain.
Watch as I lift the splinter out.
I was seven when my father
25 took my hand like this,
and I did not hold that shard
between my fingers and think,
Metal that will bury me,
christen it Little Assassin,
30 Ore Going Deep for My Heart.
And I did not lift up my wound and cry,
Death visited here!
I did what a child does
when he's given something to keep.
35 I kissed my father.

— Li-Young Lee

48 What feeling do the father's actions instill in the boy?
   1 bravery   3 wonder
   2 optimism   4 reassurance

49 The words "lovely" (line 3), "prayer" (line 8), and "tenderness" (line 10) suggest that as a child, the narrator viewed his father with an attitude of
   1 sympathy   3 astonishment
   2 adoration   4 pride

50 What feelings are revealed in lines 26 through 32?
   1 triumph and relief
   2 fear and regret
   3 peace and contentment
   4 anger and confusion

51 To what does the title of the poem most likely refer?
   1 a legacy of gentleness
   2 a capacity for storytelling
   3 an aptitude for healing
   4 a desire to help others

52 The narrator's memory of his father's actions is triggered by the situation described in
   1 line 3   3 line 9
   2 line 7   4 line 20

53 What is ironic about this poem?
   1 The father began a story but never finished it.
   2 An incident from childhood was reenacted in adulthood.
   3 The boy was injured but he did not cry.
   4 The act of removing was also an act of giving.

Passage C

For many fish species, survival means fellowship with others of their kind. The way they stick together and the varied behaviors they exhibit have delighted, perplexed, and amused observers for centuries. Some species gather in groups of no more than a half dozen and may be sociable for only a few days or weeks a year. Others spend almost
5 their entire lives swimming in formation with thousands of their fellows, packed together so tightly that they nearly rub fins as they swim.

To coordinate their activities, fishes communicate in many and sometimes most unusual ways. Some rely on sight and distinctive body-color patterns. Most have special sense organs on their skins that can "hear" the movement of their cohorts through the
10 water around them. Others talk to one another in private languages of clicks, grunts and growls. And still others communicate with electric pulses that they generate in highly specialized muscles.

Different kinds of fish schools can be both similar to and different from other kinds of animal groups Many animal societies are collections of close relatives, and members of
15 many mammal groups—such as lion prides and certain monkey troops—are at least as closely related as cousins.

Among fishes, though, familial relationships are looser. Unlike birds (and some solitary or pair-forming fish species) who feed or shelter their young, and mammals, who suckle them, schooling fishes abandon eggs and larvae to float away on the
20 currents. This drifting makes it unlikely that the fish in large schools are closely related to one another, and the lack of interaction between parents and offspring makes it equally unlikely that they themselves can tell whether they are related or not.

—Joseph S. Levine

54 According to the passage, the reason some fish congregate is for

1 territorial expansion   3 familial relationships
2 self-preservation   4 hunting efficiency

55 The phrase "half a dozen" (line 4) refers to the number of

1 observers   3   species
2 groups   4   individuals

56 In line 4, the word "sociable" is probably used to mean that the fish

1 find mates   3 migrate annually
2 live together   4 make friends

57 According to the passage, fish groups differ in
   1 location   3 swimming patterns
   2 feeding habits   4 size

58 The statement "To coordinate . . . most unusual ways"
(lines 8 and 9) is supported in the paragraph through the
use of
   1 reasons   3 examples
   2 anecdotes   4 definitions

59 According to the passage, communication among fish
sometimes relies on
   1 visual recognition   3 family relationships
   2 natural selection   4 physical contact

60 In which way are some pair-forming fishes like birds?
   1 Both build homes.
   2 Both care for their offspring.
   3 Neither interacts with parents.
   4 Neither fears mammals.

PART 2

Directions: Write a well-organized essay of about 250 words on
either *A* or *B*. [25]

A Some works of literature deal with a conflict between parent
and child. Sometimes the conflict is beneficial to the relationship; sometimes it is harmful to the relationship. From the literature you have read, choose *two* works in which a parent
and child come into conflict. For *each* work, identify the parent and child. Using specific references from *each* work, describe the conflict between the parent and child and discuss
whether the effect of the conflict on their relationship is beneficial or harmful. Give titles and authors.

B In some works of literature, an individual suffers but does not give in to despair because of some inner strength or support from others. From the literature you have read, choose *two* works in which an individual suffers yet does not despair. For *each* work, identify the individual and tell what causes the individual's suffering. Using specific references from *each* work, explain how the individual's inner strength or the support from others keeps the individual from giving in to despair. Give titles and authors.

PART 3

Directions: Answer A <u>or</u> B <u>or</u> C. [30]

A A recent letter to the editor of your local newspaper stated that after school athletic programs have little value. In a letter of about 250 words to the editor of the local newspaper, state whether you agree or disagree with the statement that after school athletic programs have little value. Support your opinion with specific reasons, examples, or details. *Write only the body of the letter.*

B More and more frequently, commercial or industrial interests come into conflict with environmental interests. Select one specific issue or situation in your region that reflects this conflict. In a 250-word article for your school newspaper, describe the issue or situation and present the arguments on both sides of the conflict. Use specific reasons, examples, or details to support your discussion.

C Write a well-organized composition of about 250 words on one of the following topics:

The fall of a hero	What I really learned in school
Organ transplants	Lost in cyberspace
Body piercing: art or vulgarity	Keeping the peace

ANSWER KEY
PRACTICE EXAM TWO

PART 1

1.	4	**21.**	1	**41.**	4
2.	3	**22.**	4	**42.**	4
3.	2	**23.**	1	**43.**	3
4.	3	**24.**	3	**44.**	3
5.	1	**25.**	2	**45.**	1
6.	4	**26.**	4	**46.**	3
7.	4	**27.**	1	**47.**	1
8.	2	**28.**	2	**48.**	4
9.	3	**29.**	4	**49.**	2
10.	1	**30.**	2	**50.**	1
11.	3	**31.**	qualify	**51.**	1
12.	2	**32.**	intellectual	**52.**	4
13.	1	**33.**	ceiling	**53.**	4
14.	1	**34.**	consciousness	**54.**	2
15.	4	**35.**	allergic	**55.**	4
16.	4	**36.**	salaries	**56.**	2
17.	1	**37.**	fragrance	**57.**	4
18.	2	**38.**	fulfill	**58.**	3
19.	1	**39.**	attendance	**59.**	1
20.	3	**40.**	vaccination	**60.**	2

ANSWERS AND EXPLANATIONS
PRACTICE EXAM TWO

PART 1

Reading Comprehension

1. 4

   1 The author mentions dense forest but nothing about steep terrain.

   2 There is no mention of this.

   3 There's no mention of what the men were wearing until about the fifth sentence, so this can't be the answer to the first question.

   4 **Correct.** "Harold and his men had marched to the village . . . straight from their battle with the Danes at Lincolnshire[.]"

2. 3

   1 The entire first paragraph is about how bedraggled Harold's army is and that it's partly made up of farmers and peasants, not soldiers.

   2 If they've just come from another battle, they can't be "untested in battle."

   3 **Correct.** "To make up for their losses at the battle they had gathered levies of men from the counties they passed through on their way south. Even so, Harold arrived at the ridge above Hastings with only a remnant of the host of men he had taken against the Danes two weeks before."

   4 The description makes you feel sorry for them. That doesn't sound like "fully equipped for battle."

3. 2

   1 What? Eliminate this immediately; it makes no sense.

   2 **Correct.** Several sentences tell you how well-fed, well-trained, and well-equipped the Normans are.

   3 Eliminate this immediately. Nothing in this section suggests that the Normans were unable to wage inland war.

   4 You should be able to eliminate this by figuring out *what the description of the Norman troops suggests*. They may have been eager to seize the hill, but that's not what these sentences are all about.

4. 3

    1 "After some discussion in the Saxon camp Harold refused the offer[.]" That's all you need to read and you get answer choice 3.

    2 "After some discussion in the Saxon camp Harold refused the offer[.]" That's all you need to read and you get answer choice 3.

    3 **Correct.** "After some discussion in the Saxon camp Harold refused the offer[.]" So King Harold broke off the negotiations.

    4 "After some discussion in the Saxon camp Harold refused the offer[.]" That's all you need to read and you get answer choice 3.

5. 1

    1 **Correct.** You have to read the phrase "he had already lost." The narrator then says, "For in the ensuing battle the Normans were to use a device of crucial significance that had been perfected in northern France over the previous hundred years." That's an important invention.

    2 The numbers and weapons of the Normans were discussed earlier in the passage, not here. Use chronology.

    3 There is no mention of discord among the troops.

    4 You may have kept this choice after the initial read-through, but if you read the phrase "he had already lost," you learned that the placement of the armies has not been discussed yet in the passage so this can't be the answer.

6. 4

    1 You may have kept this choice initially. Then in the second read-through, if you read the sentence about the beginning of the battle, you saw, "The trained men stood at the front," giving you answer choice 4. The *next* paragraph talks about the Normans' archers.

    2 You may have kept this choice initially. Then in the second read-through, if you read the sentence about the beginning of the battle, you saw, "The trained men stood at the front," giving you answer choice 4.

3 The entire paragraph is about Harold's men *not* using horses.

4 **Correct.** "As the battle began, King Harold's Saxon army was grouped along the top of the ridge . . . The trained men stood at the front[.]"

7. 4

1 Fighting on horseback meant being "prepared for flight," which means being ready to run away, being cowardly. There's no deception here, just cowardice.

2 No, the narrator says the tradition was to fight on foot.

3 If you read this part of the passage, it's at least clear that fighting on horseback meant something negative to the Saxons, so it couldn't represent nobility.

4 **Correct.** "To ride a horse into battle would have been to come to the field already prepared for flight, and such was against the Saxon battle ethic[.]" It represented cowardice.

8. 2

1 There's no mention of a predawn attack.

2 **Correct.** "At 9 a.m. the Normans advanced under a hail of arrows from their own bowmen. The plan was to break the Saxon line with the arrow strike[.]"

3 Camouflage is not mentioned.

4 There is no mention of troop division.

9. 3

1 The Saxons never retreated. Eliminate this.

2 You may have kept this initially but, on the second read-through, you should have read "the Saxons made their great mistake. They broke ranks and followed the Normans down to level ground." That's answer choice 3.

3 **Correct.** "As the Normans retreated into the valley, the Saxons made their great mistake. They broke ranks and followed the Normans down to level ground."

4 There's no mention of hurling their weapons too early.

10.   1

   1   **Correct.** "It was William's use of the stirrup to build a shock-troop of cavalry that gave him the ability to ride down the Saxons once they were on level ground."

   2   This is the last question, and the last few sentences are about the Normans winning by standing in their stirrups and "rid[ing] down" the Saxons. No arrows figure here.

   3   This is the last question, and the last few sentences are about the Normans winning by standing in their stirrups and "rid[ing] down" the Saxons.

   4   This is the last question, and the last few sentences are about the Normans winning by standing in their stirrups and "rid[ing] down" the Saxons.

Vocabulary

11.   3   *Compulsion* should remind you of the word *compelled*, which means "feeling a strong drive to do something." So, *compulsion* must mean something like a strong drive. The closest thing is choice 3, "strong impulse."

12.   2   *Laden* means "loaded" or "burdened."

13.   1   Have you ever heard the term "unconditional love"? That's love that won't disappear no matter what happens. So, *unconditionally* must mean something not disappearing no matter what happens. Choice 1, "absolutely," is the closest thing you've got.

14.   1   From expressions such as "dire need," "dire threat," and "dire circumstances," you probably know that *dire* is an extremely negative word. The only extremely negative answer choice is 1, "dreadful."

15.   4   When something is mandatory, you have to do it. So, a mandate must be something that you have to do or a command.

16.   4   Have you ever heard someone exclaim, "I can't believe you'd have the audacity to say . . ." If so, you can eliminate choices 1 and 2, because you know that you need a negative word.

17.   1   You may have heard of someone's being "granted a reprieve" and know that this is a positive thing. If so, you can eliminate choices 2 and 4. Could someone be granted an unlawful escape? Sounds funky, so eliminate choice 3 as well.

18. 2 You've probably heard this word used to mean to kick a president out of office. "Kick out of office" isn't an answer choice, but no matter: Think about what's entailed in kicking a president out of office. Libel? No, that's telling damaging lies about someone, which wouldn't necessarily be part of an impeachment. Accuse? Sure, it makes sense that you couldn't impeach a president without accusing him or her of doing something wrong. Defeat? That sounds more like a losing campaign than an impeachment. Punish? Maybe. So, eliminate choices 1 and 3.

19. 1 *Conversely* means "the opposite of."

20. 3 *To transpire* means "to happen, to occur." "I don't know if I'll be able to go to the party tonight. I have to go home and see what transpires when my mom sees my report card."

21. 1 You may have heard the word *prefabricated*, which means getting "something for which all the parts were made beforehand" (e.g., a house, a sandwich), so that the builder just has to piece them all together. Because you know that the prefix *pre-* means "before," then *fabricated* must mean something like made. The closest thing is choice 1, "created."

22. 4 You've no doubt only heard this word used to describe someone who's walking on the street. Although this is not the meaning on which you are being tested here, you can still use this knowledge to get you to the answer. Could you describe your average person on the street as ridiculous? Not unless you have a really strange perspective. Childish? No. Disturbing? No. Ordinary? Well, yeah, that's the point. So, answer choice 4 it is.

23. 1 If you know that *apprehensively* is a negative word, you can eliminate answer choice 2.

24. 3 This word may remind you of the word *emphasize*, which means "to express strongly." Therefore, *emphatically* probably means something like strongly expressed. Choice 3, "forcefully," is the best guess.

25. 2 You may have heard the word *tedious*, which means "boring." From that, you can guess that tedium is boredom.

26. 4 You may recognize *append* as part of *appendix*. What's an appendix? It's something added onto the end of a book or report. So, *append* must mean "to add onto" or "attach."

27. 1 You may have heard the word *scrutinize*, which means "to examine something very closely," so scrutiny is careful examination. Also, out of all the answer choices, number 4, "continuous patrol" makes the least sense in the sentence, so you could eliminate that.

28. 2 To find something plausible is to believe it.

29. 4 To consolidate means to combine several separate things into one unit. Note the prefix, *con-*, which means "together."

30. 2 You may have heard the word *ineptitude*. Most likely you've heard it applied to someone who's incompetent to do his or her job. So, *inept* probably means "incompetent" or "unfit."

Spelling

31. qualify

32. intellectual

33. ceiling

34. consciousness

35. allergic

36. salaries

37. fragrance

38. fulfill

39. attendance

40. vaccination

41. 4

1 "Barely Berlitz version" refers to how they spoke the language. "Dizzy" has nothing to do with the language: It's how they felt after walking a lot.

2 They spoke a "barely Berlitz version" of the language. "Stared" describes how they looked at the other visitors; it has nothing to do with the language.

3 "Barely Berlitz version" describes how they spoke the language. "Visitors" are just the other people at whom they stared; this word has nothing to do with the language.

4 **Correct.** Even if you don't know that Berlitz is a travel language guide, you do know that "barely Berlitz version" refers to how they spoke the language. "Stammered" is the only one of the answer choices that also refers to how they spoke the language.

42. 4

1 Courage is not mentioned in this section.

2 Although "sensual style" (line 7) is mentioned in passing, this section is not primarily about fashion.

3 "Romance" is not quite right. Although Paris is described as "seductive" (line 6) and "sensual" (line 7), this is not the main idea of this section.

4 **Correct.** This section is all about celebrating the French Revolution and "Liberty, Equality, Fraternity" (lines 9–10). It is about freedom.

43. 3

1 There's no sadness mentioned in this paragraph.

2 Time isn't mentioned in this section.

3 **Correct.** The narrator tells us that "it was dark" (line 11) but that the cathedral glowed in a "wash of artificial, mellow light" (line 13).

4 This is too much of a leap. The author doesn't talk about stability and change in this paragraph.

44. 3

    1 The narrator never says that they'd become best friends.

    2 The narrator doesn't mention speaking French in this section.

    3 **Correct.** The narrator is happy that she and her companions "could find and trust each other enough to travel together into a land where none of us belonged" (lines 19–20).

    4 There's nothing said about an anniversary.

45. 1

    1 **Correct.** In the paragraph before this, the narrator describes how a group of black women were having no problems traveling in Paris. The fifth paragraph starts, "But then we tried to get a cab . . ." (line 22), suggesting that this experience made her think that there was prejudice in Paris (among the cab drivers) after all.

    2 Only one of the cab drivers is reckless; the others just refuse to stop for a group of black women.

    3 There's nothing here about dishonesty.

    4 Only one of the cab drivers drives irresponsibly; the others just refuse to pick up the group.

46. 3

    1 *Perplexed* means "confused." During her last hours in Paris, the narrator knows exactly how she feels.

    2 The narrator never says anything about being frightened.

    3 **Correct.** The words "miserable" (line 26) and "trashed our holiday confidence and joy" (line 31) let you know that the narrator was feeling disheartened.

    4 The narrator is clearly upset, but there is no evidence that she is angry.

47. 1

    1 **Correct.** In this line, the author seems to be defending herself against something negative someone has said or thought about her. We don't know what that something is until we hear about the taxi experience.

    2 These lines are pure happiness. There's nothing in them to fore-shadow the negative experience to come.

    3 These lines are all about pleasure. They don't hint at the bad time to come.

4 These lines just describe the group. They don't make us think that anything bad is coming.

48. 4

1 The actions don't make the narrator feel brave.

2 There's nothing here to suggest that his father's actions make the narrator optimistic.

3 The narrator never says that the actions made him feel wonder. In fact, in lines 6–7, the author says that he remembers his father's voice but that the story itself didn't make an impression on him.

4 **Correct.** The father told the narrator a story to calm and distract him—that is, to reassure him—while he took out the narrator's splinter.

49. 2

1 Nothing happens to the father to elicit feelings of sympathy.

2 **Correct.** These words make it clear how absolutely crazy about his father the narrator was.

3 There's nothing here to suggest that the narrator was surprised by his father; the father did exactly what the narrator expected that he would do.

4 Although the narrator obviously adored his father, he says nothing with these words about being proud of him.

50. 1

1 **Correct.** What's going on in these lines? The narrator's father has just taken the splinter out. What emotions does he describe? Well, in lines 31–32 he talks about lifting his wound in the air and yelling about how he defeated death (there's your triumph), and in lines 26–30, he talks about looking at the shard, now outside his body, and thinking about how it could have killed him (there's your relief).

2 There is no cause for regret or fear in these lines: The splinter has just been taken out.

3 In lines 31–32, the narrator describes lifting up his wound and yelling. This does not sound very peaceful.

4 There is no anger or confusion here. The narrator's just happy that the splinter is out.

51. 1

    1 **Correct.** The poem is about a father taking out a son's splinter gently and about the son growing up to be able to take his wife's splinter out just as gently. A legacy is something that is handed down from generation to generation, so it makes sense to say that "The Gift" is a legacy of gentleness.

    2 This poem is not about storytelling. The narrator never tells us that the son inherited the gift of storytelling.

    3 This is close but not quite right. The father doesn't heal the son; he just takes a splinter out of his hand. The father's real gift, which he passes on to the son, is his gentleness.

    4 We don't know whether either the father or the son has a desire to help others in general; all we know is that they are very gentle with close family members.

52. 4

    1 This is part of the actual memory, not the trigger for the memory.

    2 This is part of the narrator's memory, not the situation that triggered the memory.

    3 This is part of the memory, not the trigger for the memory.

    4 **Correct.** This line is about the narrator taking a splinter out of his wife's hand. Within this stanza, the narrator starts talking again about his father taking the splinter out when he was a kid. From this, we can infer that the narrator's removal of the splinter from his wife's hand triggered the memory.

53. 4

    1 Irony is language that conveys a certain idea by saying just the opposite. There's nothing ironic about not finishing a story.

    2 Irony is language that conveys a certain idea by saying just the opposite. There is nothing ironic about this.

    3 Irony is language that conveys a certain idea by saying just the opposite. There's nothing ironic about a kid's not crying when he's hurt.

    4 **Correct.** Irony is language that conveys a certain idea by saying just the opposite. This is ironic because, while the poem describes the father *removing* a splinter, what was really happening was that the father was *giving* the son the gift of gentleness.

54. 2

    1 There's nothing here about territorial expansion.

    2 **Correct.** In the first line, the author says "survival means fellow-ship with others of their kind." In other words, they congregate for self-preservation.

    3 Stick with the beginning of the passage. Familial relationships aren't mentioned until much later on.

    4 Hunting is never mentioned.

55. 4

    1 The observers in line 3 are people; the groups of "half a dozen" are fish.

    2 Read carefully. There aren't "half a dozen" groups; there are "half a dozen" fish per group.

    3 Don't be fooled just because "species" is the last thing mentioned before "half a dozen." Half a dozen refers to the number of fish in a group made up of one species.

    4 **Correct.** "Half a dozen" is the number of individual fish in a group. Remember, we're talking about fish's "fellowship with others of their kind" (line 1), so the "groups of no more than half a dozen" would have to be individuals of the same kind of fish.

56. 2

    1 Get your mind out of the gutter, will you? We're not talking about mating here. We're talking about fish hanging out in groups.

    2 **Correct.** In line 3, the author says that fish "gather in groups." So, we can assume that "sociable" means that the fish gather in groups or live together.

    3 There is nothing here about migration.

    4 It would be a little silly to decide that the little fish were friends. All we know is that they hang out in a group.

57. 4

    1 No specific locations are mentioned.

    2 The author doesn't describe any feeding habits.

    3 The author never compares different groups' swimming patterns.

4 **Correct.** Using chronology, you know that the answer to this question is probably somewhere before line 8 (the line reference for the next question). And sure enough, the author says "Some species gather in groups of no more than half a dozen . . . Others spend almost their entire lives . . . with thousands of their fellows" (lines 3–6).

58. 3

1 The author never gives any motivations for the fish's unusual ways of coordinating their activities; he just describes them.

2 Anecdotes are stories. The author doesn't tell any stories in this section.

3 **Correct.** The author talks about "sight and distinctive body-color patterns" (line 9), "special sense organs on their skins" (line 10), "private languages" (lines 11–12), and "electric pulses" (lines 12–13), all examples of the ways that fish communicate.

4 The author gives no definitions in this section.

59. 1

1 **Correct.** You don't have to hunt too much for this answer, because it's right in the same section where you went looking for the answer to the last question. In line 9, the author says that, to communicate, some fish "rely on sight and distinctive body-color patterns."

2 The author never mentions natural selection.

3 The ways that fish communicate is mentioned in line 8. Family relationships aren't discussed until line 18. Look for an answer choice earlier in the passage.

4 Physical contact is never mentioned.

60. 2

1 Look for the words "birds" and "pair-forming fish": You'll find the first in line 18 and the second in line 19. Do you see anything here about home building? No. We know that these fish shelter their young, but we don't know whether the fish build the shelters themselves.

2 **Correct.** You'll find the word "birds" in line 18 and "pair-forming fish" in line 19. The author says about them that they both "feed or shelter their young" (line 19). This is a good paraphrase for caring for their offspring.

3   The author say about birds and some pair-forming fish that they "feed or shelter their young" (line 19). This suggests that the young do interact with their parents.

4   Use common sense on this one: Birds don't fear mammals? Any bird that doesn't fear mammals such as cats isn't going to live long.

PART 2

Essay A

Score: 84 percent

Some works of literature deal with a conflict between parent and child. In certain cases this conflict has tragic results. Two examples of this are Shakespeare's *Romeo and Juliet* and Arthur Miller's *Death of a Salesman*.

In *Romeo and Juliet,* Juliet comes into conflict with her father, Capulet, over marrying Paris. Capulet insists that Juliet must marry Paris, threatening to throw Juliet out and disown her if she refuses. Juliet feels that there is no way out so she agrees to the scheme that eventually leaves both her and Romeo, the boy she loves, dead. After finding Juliet dead, Capulet sees the error of his ways, and agrees to end the feud that led to his daughter's death. So, although the conflict ultimately has the positive effect of ending the long and pointless feud that has killed members of both the Capulet and Montague families, it is still far more negative than positive, leaving Juliet dead, and Capulet without his daughter.

In *Death of a Salesman,* Biff, Willy Loman's older son, comes into conflict with his father because Willy has always insisted upon seeing Biff as faultless. Willy tries to make his son fulfill his own desire for success. In a flashback, Willy rationalizes Biff's theft of a football as a teenager, and exaggerates Biff's athletic talent. Finally, as an adult, Biff explodes under the pressure of his father's unrealistic expectations, and confesses all of his faults to his father. This proves to be the last straw for Willy, who gets into his car and crashes it at full speed, killing himself. In the last scene, at Willy's funeral, Biff realizes that he can finally face who he is, and start to work toward being his own person. This is a positive effect, but it doesn't outweigh the tragedy of Willy's death over a conflict with his son that should have been resolved long before.

The relationships between parents and children will always include conflict. Yet, as we see from *Romeo and Juliet* and *Death of a Salesman*, such conflict must be kept under control, or tragedy can result.

Comments

The writer should have described the two conflicts in the first paragraph, and then in the second and third paragraphs given more details about the conflicts. In the second paragraph, rather than referring to "the scheme," the writer should have given concrete details—that Juliet and Romeo married secretly and that Juliet was then to drink the sleeping potion, etc. The third paragraph gives a slightly inaccurate impression by implying that Willy kills himself as a direct result of his conflict with Biff, when in reality he has planned this suicide for some time, for the insurance money. It would show a better understanding of the text if the writer explained that Willy's intentions in committing suicide were to help Biff and to preserve his own dream.

PART 3

Composition C

Score: 93 percent

Body Piercing: Art or Vulgarity

For a teenager, I have a surprisingly good relationship with my mother. We usually even agree on movies and music. The only time that we almost killed each other was when I told her that I wanted to get my bellybutton pierced.

I have never seen my mother get so upset about something. Once the dust cleared, and she stopped yelling things like "trashy," "ugly" and "tasteless," I saw that she had three main reasons for objecting. First, she thought that it was wrong to "defile my body." Second, she thought that it was stupid to do something permanent like piercing my body just because it was in style this year. Third, she just thought it was ugly and vulgar-looking.

I listened to everything my mother had to say without screaming back or crying. Then I tried to answer each of her arguments. The "defiling my body" argument did not make sense because my mother has pierced ears. This changes her body as much as a bellybutton piercing would change mine. Besides, didn't we "defile our bodies" every time we cut our hair or shaved our legs or even put on makeup? Her second argument, that piercing is permanent, is not necessarily true. One friend of mine had to have her naval ring taken out when she got her appendix out, and the hole closed up within a couple of weeks. Although piercings may look permanent, they do not have to be. Her third agument was just that it was vulgar and ugly. I told her that, although to her generation body piercing is vulgar, to mine it looks good and it is not even that radical. One generation's vulgarity is another generation's body art.

The happy ending is that my mother let me do it. I love my bellybutton ring and my mother still hates it. To her it's vulgarity but she understands that to me it is art.

Comments

The essay is very well organized, although the tone is somewhat flat. The points are good and clearly stated.

ABOUT THE AUTHOR

Gabrielle Maisels attended Harvard and Columbia and joined The Princeton Review in 1993. She is the co-creator of the Review's new LSAT course, a Licensed Massage Therapist, and author of *Cracking the Regents: Comprehensive English.*

Free!

Did you know that The Microsoft Network gives you one free month?

Call us at 1-800-FREE MSN. We'll send you a free CD to get you going.

Then, you can explore the World Wide Web for one month, free. Exchange e-mail with your family and friends. Play games, book airline tickets, handle finances, go car shopping, explore old hobbies and discover new ones. There's one big, useful online world out there. And for one month, it's a free world.

Call **1-800-FREE MSN,** Dept. 3197, for offer details or visit us at **www.msn.com**. Some restrictions apply.

Microsoft Where do you want to go today?®   **MSn**™
The Microsoft Network

FIND US...

International

Hong Kong
4/F Sun Hung Kai Centre
30 Harbour Road, Wan Chai,
Hong Kong
Tel: (011)85-2-517-3016

Japan
Fuji Building 40, 15-14
Sakuragaokacho, Shibuya Ku,
Tokyo 150, Japan
Tel: (011)81-3-3463-1343

Korea
Tae Young Bldg, 944-24,
Daechi- Dong, Kangnam-Ku
The Princeton Review- ANC
Seoul, Korea 135-280,
South Korea
Tel: (011)82-2-554-7763

Mexico City
PR Mex S De RL De Cv
Guanajuato 228 Col. Roma
06700 Mexico D.F., Mexico
Tel: 525-564-9468

Montreal
666 Sherbrooke St.
West, Suite 202
Montreal, QC H3A 1E7 Canada
Tel: (514) 499-0870

Pakistan
1 Bawa Park - 90 Upper Mall
Lahore, Pakistan
Tel: (011)92-42-571-2315

Spain
Pza. Castilla, 3 - 5° A, 28046
Madrid, Spain
Tel: (011)341-323-4212

Taiwan
155 Chung Hsiao East Road
Section 4 - 4th Floor,
Taipei R.O.C., Taiwan
Tel: (011)886-2-751-1243

Thailand
Building One, 99 Wireless Road
Bangkok, Thailand 10330
Tel: (662) 256-7080

Toronto
1240 Bay Street, Suite 300
Toronto M5R 2A7 Canada
Tel: (800) 495-7737
Tel: (716) 839-4391

Vancouver
4212 University Way NE,
Suite 204
Seattle, WA 98105
Tel: (206) 548-1100

locations

National (U.S.)

We have over 60 offices around the U.S. and
run courses in over 400 sites. For courses and locations
within the U.S. call 1 (800) 2/Review and you will be
routed to the nearest office.